Metamorphoses

To Colette,
queen of metamorphoses

Metamorphoses

Emanuele Coccia

Translated by Robin Mackay

polity

Originally published in French as *Métamorphoses* © 2020, Éditions Payot & Rivages

This English translation © 2021, Polity Press

Polity Press
65 Bridge Street
Cambridge CB2 1UR, UK

Polity Press
101 Station Landing
Suite 300
Medford, MA 02155, USA

ISBN-13: 978-1-5095-4566-7
ISBN-13: 978-1-5095-4567-4 (paperback)

A catalogue record for this book is available from the British Library.

Library of Congress Cataloging-in-Publication Data

Names: Coccia, Emanuele, author. | Mackay, Robin (Philosopher), translator.

Title: Metamorphoses / Emanuele Coccia ; translated by Robin Mackay.
Other titles: Métamorphoses. English
Description: Cambridge, UK ; Medford, MA, USA : Polity Press, 2021. | Translation of: Métamorphoses. | Includes bibliographical references. | Summary: "A brilliant reflection on the interconnectedness of all life"-- Provided by publisher.
Identifiers: LCCN 2020055364 (print) | LCCN 2020055365 (ebook) | ISBN 9781509545667 (hardback) | ISBN 9781509545674 (paperback) | ISBN 9781509545681 (epub) | ISBN 9781509547685 (pdf)
Subjects: LCSH: Transmigration. | Life. | Ecology.
Classification: LCC BD426 .C6313 2021 (print) | LCC BD426 (ebook) | DDC 129--dc23
LC record available at https://lccn.loc.gov/2020055364
LC ebook record available at https://lccn.loc.gov/2020055365

Typeset in 11 on 14 pt Sabon by
Servis Filmsetting Ltd, Stockport, Cheshire
Printed and bound in Great Britain by TJ Books Ltd, Padstow, Cornwall

For further information on Polity, visit our website: politybooks.com

Contents

Acknowledgements

I have often been told that the second birth is far less painful than the first. The mother's body has learned from its past experience and can perform the necessary movements more easily and quickly. I have also often been told that writing a book is a kind of childbirth. My body does not have, and never will have, the ability to carry a child, so I cannot comment on the legitimacy of this comparison or on the second birth. What I do know is that writing a book has always been a painful and unpredictable experience for me. In writing, no accumulation of experience is possible: no knowhow, no mastery. Faced with the book, any book, I am, and always have been, a clumsy dilettante, and I have always felt like a child facing an unknown object with a magical allure, who doesn't really understand how it works. Faced with this, the closeness of friends with whom I can chat and spend time is the only form of epidural anaesthesia. Frédérique Aït-Touati reread several versions of the book and generously discussed many of the ideas contained herein: my dialogue with her and with her work has been essential, and I want to thank her with all my heart. My dialogue with Bruno Latour has enabled me to progress on many points: I am extremely grateful to him.

This book affirms the unity of all living beings present, future, and past, and the unity of the living being with the matter of the world: this is what has often been called pantheism. Discussions over time with Giorgio Agamben have left a deep impression upon me. Emanuele Dattilo is writing a book on this hidden tradition and its repressed history.

The book could not have been born without all that I was able to learn from conversations woven across time with Adel Abdessemed, Léonore Bancilhon, Marcello Barison, Rocio Berenguer Soldan, Stefano Boeri, Bianca Bondi, Chiara Bottici, Giovanni Careri, Barbara Carnevali, Lucien Castaing-Taylor, Dorothée Charles, Emanuele Clarizio, Gilles Clément, Michela Coccia, Veronica Dari, Laetitia Dosch, Simone Farresin, Donatien Grau, Sabine Guermouche, Camille Henrot, Noreen Khawaja, Sophie Kurkdjian Nadia Yala Kisuki, Mathilde Laurent, Alice Leroy, Fabian Ludueña Romandini, Filippo Mignini, Jeremy Narby, Ernesto Neto, Hans Ulrich Obrist, Verena Paravel, Philippe Parreno, Éric Philippe, Christine Rebet, Massimo Scolaro, Bas Smets, Michele Spanò, Andrea Trimarchi, Éloïse van der Heyden, Chiara Vecchiarelli, Marie Vic, Barbara Vinken, Caterina Zanfi, and Luis Zerbini.

In addition to people, this book has been made possible thanks to the cities where I have had the chance to stay for various periods.

In Paris, during the final months of the writing process, I had the opportunity to collaborate in the organization of an exhibition about trees at the Fondation Cartier: the writing of the book came out of the experience completely transformed. I thank Hervé Chandes for this invitation and for the important discussions I had with him, Pierre-Édouard Couton, Isabelle Gaudefroid, Adeline Pelletier, and Marie Perennes. A striking remark by Bruce Albers on the eighth floor of the Fondation was decisive: I especially thank him.

In Karlsruhe, invited by Bruno Latour to give a lecture, an advance version of the manuscript and three years of work melted in a few drops of coffee. It was one of the most radical and happy rejuvenative experiences of recent years: the book would certainly have been different without this involuntary metamorphosis.

In Monaco, the dialogues opened up with Charlotte Casiraghi, Joseph Cohen, Roger-Pol Droit, Laura Hugo, Robert Maggiori, and Raphael Zaguri-Orly have punctuated my intellectual life for the past three years: I would like to thank them for their generosity and their ability to bring thought everywhere.

In Brussels, Laurent van Eynde allowed me to present a first version of the book, and to discuss it with Natacha Pfeiffer and Maud Hagelstein.

In London, I was able to discuss a few pages of the book with Filipa Ramos, Lucia Pietroiusti, Martin Savranski, and John Tresch.

Many of the ideas in this book were born during a short stay in Wellington made possible by Stéphane Re: meeting him and Alizée Alexandre was very important.

In Curitiba, I was able to present and discuss in detail a first draft with Alexandre Nodari, Juliana Fausta, Juliàn Nowodworski, Marco Antonio Valentim, and Flavia Cera.

In Rio de Janeiro, Anna Dantes, Madeleine Deschamps, Marcus Wagner, and the entire Selvagem team welcomed the ideas in the book with great generosity and passion.

In New York, Phillip Usher, Meriam Korichi, and

Omar Berrada helped me move forward with the writing of the book.

By a strange coincidence, I must have written a good part of the text in Weimar, a few hundred metres from the place where Goethe composed his writings on the metamorphosis of plants. I am profoundly grateful to Bernard Siegert and Lorenz Engell for welcoming me to the IKKM, and to Leander Scholz, Elena Vogmann, and Katarzyna Włoszczyńska for the discussions.

I would like to thank my editor, Lidia Breda, who always knows how to alternate between pressure and attentiveness with an art that is hers alone. Renaud Paquette was the first reader of the manuscript: his remarks and suggestions made it possible to considerably improve the text by carrying out the very last metamorphosis of the manuscript. I am extremely grateful to him.

Maria Assunta Tosoni and Michele Coccia, my mother and father, taught me from childhood not to be afraid of any kind of metamorphosis. I thank them for their courage, their freedom, their madness.

I dedicate this book to my daughter Colette. She arrived barely five years ago and she has changed everything around her, and around me: she has lit up the worlds through which she has travelled with a joy and grace I had never before encountered. She knows all the secrets of metamorphosis – and she has revealed a few of them to me.

I am everything because I am only the stream of life, free of accident. I am immortal because all deaths converge in me, from that of the fish to that of Zeus; gathered in me they once again become life, not individual and particular but belonging to nature and thus free.

Giuseppe Tomasi di Lampedusa

INTRODUCTION

The Continuity of Life

In the beginning we were all the same living creature, sharing the same body and the same experience. And things haven't changed so much since then. New forms and new modes of existence have proliferated. But even today, we are all still the same life. For millions of years this life has been transmitted from body to body, from individual to individual, from species to species, from kingdom to kingdom. Of course it shifts, it transforms. But the life of each living being does not begin with its own birth: it is far older than that.

Take our own existence. Our life, what we imagine to be the most intimate and incommunicable part of ourselves, does not come from us, and there is nothing exclusive or personal about it: it was transmitted to us by others, it has animated other bodies, chunks of matter different from the one in which we are currently harboured. For nine months, the fact that the life that animates and awakens us has no one name or owner was an obvious physical, material fact. We were the same body, the same humours, the same atoms as our mother. And we are that life, shared with the body of another, carried on and taken elsewhere.

It is the breath of another that is continued in ours, the blood of another that flows through our veins; it is the DNA we have received from another that sculpts and shapes our body. Just as our life begins long before we are born, it does not end until well after our death. The breath of life will not expire in our corpse: it will go on to feed those for whom we will become a festive Last Supper.

Nor is our humanity something originary and autonomous. The human, also, is but a continuation and metamorphosis of a life that came before it. More precisely, it is an invention which primates, another life form, drew out of their own bodies – from their life force, their DNA, their way of life – so as to enable the life that inhabited and animated them to exist in a different form. They transmitted this form to us and, through the human life form, they continue to live within us. And even the primates themselves are just an experiment, a wager on the part of yet other species, yet other life forms. Evolution is a masquerade that takes place in time rather than in space. A masquerade that allows each species, from one era to the next, to don a new mask, different from the one that engendered it; that allows sons and daughters to pass unrecognized by and to no longer recognize their parents. And yet, despite this changing of masks, mother-species and daughter-species are metamorphoses of the self-same life. Each species is a patchwork of parts taken from other species. We, the living species, have continually exchanged parts, lineages, organs; what each of us is, what we call our 'species', is only a set of techniques that each living being has borrowed from others. It is because of this continuity-in-transformation that every species shares infinitely many traits with hundreds of other species. The fact that we have eyes, ears, lungs, noses, warm blood

– this is something we have in common with millions of other individuals, thousands of other species – and in all of these traits we are only ever partly human. Every species is the metamorphosis of all those that preceded it. One and the same life, cobbling together a new body, a new form, in order to exist differently.

This is the deepest meaning of the Darwinian theory of evolution, the one that biology and pop science don't want to think about: species are not substances or real entities. They are 'life games' (in the same sense as 'language games'): unstable and necessarily ephemeral configurations of a life that likes to transit and circulate from one form to another. We have not yet grasped the full consequences of Darwin's intuition: to say that species are connected by a genetic relationship does not simply mean that living creatures make up one vast family or clan. Above all, it means realizing that the identity of each species is entirely relative: primates may be the parents and humans their children, but we are human only through and in relation to those early primates, just as each of us is not a daughter or son in an absolute sense, but only in relation to our mother and father. Any species identity only describes a particular configuration of continuity (and metamorphosis) with other species.

All of the above also applies to living creatures taken as a whole. There is no opposition between the living and the non-living. Not only is every living creature continuous with the non-living, it is its extension, metamorphosis, and most extreme expression.

Life is always the reincarnation of that which is not alive, a cobbling together of mineral elements, a carnival of the telluric substance of a planet – Gaia, the Earth – which continually presents new faces and creates new modes of being out of even the smallest particle of its disparate, heteroclite body. Every self is a vehicle for the Earth, a vessel that allows the planet to travel without moving.

The Forms within Us

It was long before the era of social networks. Photos of oneself were few and far between; they saved rare moments from oblivion, absorbing into themselves the colour and light of the life that they incarnated. They were kept in large, bound albums with white pages that were rarely flipped through and even less frequently shown to others – as if they were sacred tomes that could only be revealed to the initiated. These albums didn't usually contain any writing, but they presupposed long oral explanations. For plunging into their pages meant each time rediscovering the evidence of a past that one would rather forget.

Upon these pages, life took the form of a long parade of autonomous silhouettes separated by great halos of darkness. In spite of the dissimilarity of the forms, it was not difficult to recognize oneself in this strange parade of exuviae from our past. And yet a certain frisson accompanied this succession of characters ready to say 'I' in our place. Apparently cancelling out all difference in time, the album seemed to exhibit these images as in a polyptych of a large extended family: with a strange dissociative effect, it transformed them into almost identical twins who seemed to be leading parallel lives. So that our existence began to seem like a titanic effort to pass from one life to another, from one form to another – a journey of reincarnation through bodies and situations far removed from one another, as the cockroach is from Gregor Samsa's human body. But then at other times, on the contrary, the magic worked in the opposite direction: to leaf through the album was to experience the intoxication of a perfect equivalence between the most disparate forms. Without being completely identical, our current self revealed itself to be exactly the same one as when we were only one metre tall, barely able to peer above the stalks in a cornfield; or when we were a teenager with bad hair and an acne-riddled face. The differences were enormous, and yet each of these forms expressed the same life with the same force. Such albums are the most accurate representation of the coincidence between life and metamorphosis.

We are always struck by the form of the living being at the adult age. In the body at this stage we recognize a perfection and maturity that we deny to others. Everything that goes before is seen as mere preparation for this silhouette we were destined to inhabit, and all that follows is decadence and decline. Yet nothing could be further from the truth. Our adult life form is no more perfect, no more 'us', no more human, no more complete than that of the bicellular embryo that comes directly after the fertilization of the egg, or that of the old man on the verge of death. All life, in order to develop, must pass through an irreducible multiplicity of forms, a whole population of bodies that it dons and discards with the same ease as it changes outfits from one season to the next. Every living being is legion. Each one stitches together bodies and 'selves' like a seamstress, like a body artist constantly modifying their appearance. Every life is an anatomical fashion show of variable duration.

To think the relationship between this multiplicity of forms in terms of metamorphosis rather than in terms of evolution, progress, or their opposites, is not just to free oneself of all teleology. It means also, and above all, that each of these forms has the same weight, the same importance, the same value: metamorphosis is the principle of equivalence between all natures, and the process that allows this equivalence to arise. Every form, every nature, comes from the other and is equivalent to it. They all exist on the same plane. They each have a share of what the others have, but in different ways. Variation is *horizontal*.

It isn't easy to hold the gaze of this liturgy of silhouettes, none of which seems capable of both retaining and modifying the life that has been transmitted to it. In this incessant carnival of figures at once rubbing shoulders with one another contemporaneously and constituting a line of succession, forms fade into one another, pour into one another, engender one another. Each of them is a stranger that seems to come from elsewhere but who, once we become familiar with them, makes all the others seem like strangers. What we call life – whether from the point of view of the individual, the species, or the kingdoms as a whole – is nothing but a process of the domestication of successive forms. Day after day we domesticate the stranger, to the point where we lose ourselves completely in their body.

Let us call metamorphosis this twofold self-evident truth: every living thing is in itself a plurality of forms – simultaneously present and successive – but none of these forms truly exists autonomously and separately, because they are always defined in immediate continuity with an infinite number of others that come before and after. Metamorphosis is both the force that allows every living thing to be staged simultaneously and successively across several forms, and the breath of life that connects those forms with one another, allowing them to pass one into the other.

1

BIRTHS

Every Self is a Forgetting

Like everyone else, I have forgotten. The taste and smell of that moment, the people around me, the objects in the room. I don't remember the day or the time, what my thoughts and emotions were, the intensity of the light in those very first moments. Perhaps I had to forget? Everything was appearing to me for the first time: too different, too new, too intense for me to take stock of it. I had to forget – forget everything. Become empty so as to make space for everything else: for what was yet to come, for what would soon be my past, for the whole world. I had to clear a space in order for any experience to be possible. I had to forget, and forget everything, to be able to perceive myself.

Birth is the absolute limit of recognition. It is the threshold where to say 'I' is to fuse with another. Impossible to say whether the breath that allows us to pronounce this syllable truly belongs to us or whether it is a continuation of our mother's body; impossible to say whether this syllable names our body or the one from which we emerge. Birth is the force that allows us to say 'I' only if we negate all memory: we must forget where we come from, we must forget the other body that sheltered us for so long, we must de-identify ourselves from it.

Like everyone else, I have forgotten. I have forgotten myself, but above all I have forgotten everything that lived within me and continues to live within me. For instance, I have forgotten that for nine months I was inside my mother's body. Not just inside her, I *was* her body, literally. I was a part of her womb, materially inseparable from it. Flesh of her flesh, life of her life. This forgetting is not accidental, it is the condition of possibility for beginning to see oneself differently. It is the cognitive counterpart of the act of becoming other than one's mother, of continuing her life and her breath apart from her womb and her consciousness.

Like everyone else, I have forgotten that I was my father's body. I was and still am; and not just from a material point of view. By birth, I carry within me the form of my father and the form of my mother: genetically, I am the improbable and noisy dialogue between their bodies and their forms. This forgetfulness that coincides with birth is the deepest part of memory. And of course my parents too are the fruit of the same oblivion and fusion. To have within me the body of my father and mother, to have their forms, their life, therefore means having within me the body and the life of an innumerable series of living beings, all born of other living beings, stretching out to the borders of humanity and beyond, to the frontiers of the living, and even further. Birth is not simply the emergence of the new, it is also the erratic wandering of the future through a limitless past.

Like everyone else, I have forgotten. I couldn't have done otherwise. I had to forget everything in order to become what I am. Being born means forgetting that we were something before, forgetting that the other continues to live within us. We were there already, but in a different form: birth is not an absolute beginning. There was already something before us, we were already something before being born, there was something of me there before I existed. And this is what birth is: the impossibility of ever stepping outside the relation of continuity between our self and the self of others, between human and non-human life, between life and the matter that makes up the world.

I was born. I am always a vessel for something other than myself. The self is only a vehicle for foreign matter which comes from elsewhere and is destined to go on elsewhere without me, whether it's words, smells, visions, or molecules.

I was born. There is nothing purely present in the matter of which I am made. I am a vehicle of the ancestral past, destined for an unimaginable future. I am a motley, irreconcilable temporality that cannot be pinned down to any epoch or moment. I am a reaction between many disparate moments on the surface of Gaia.

I was born – it's almost a tautology. To become an 'I' is to be born, and being born is the dynamism that defines every I. Only beings that are born have an 'I' – or, conversely, the 'I' is only a vehicle: it always transports something other than itself.

One and the Same Life

We describe it as the process that connects parents with their children. We imagine that in this process bodies are ordered according to specific relationships, and describe the result as a succession of generations – from mothers and fathers to daughters and sons. We imagine it as something from which there sprouts a gigantic tree whose branches stretch out to take in cousins, uncles, aunts, grandparents, and those relatives for whom we have no names to define our degree of kinship but whom we loosely call our extended family. We speak of the bonds of flesh and blood. But we forget the strangest thing about birth: life is constituted in a way that is both far more outlandish and far more intimate than our makeshift concepts would have us believe.

Look at our children: a part of our body has become other. First of all, it joined with a foreign body and engendered another life, autonomous and separate from us. The same could be said of consciousness. A part of our ego escaped us and became other, disconnected from us. Our self now exists outside us, distinct from us, forever out of reach. This other life that was once ours says 'I' just as we do, and it is literally the same piece of mind and matter that was our own 'I' and that of our partner. And yet this life unfolds elsewhere, on, in, and through another body or, to put it another way, within our own body and mind become other.

Every child is an unrecognizable self. Every child is a body that has operated a metamorphosis on the matter from which it originated. The multiplication of bodies and selves – what we call being born – is first of all a process of the transformation of existing bodies. What we experience as forgetting, as an unsurpassable limit of recognition and memory, is a metamorphosis. By virtue of its birth every living body, regardless of its form, dimensions, and situation, but also regardless of the species and kingdom to which it belongs, is a metamorphosis: a transformation of previous bodies, a modification of a form that existed before it, a mutation of a way of looking at things that had already made a difference to the world.

If we are born, it is because each one of us, in body and soul alike, is only one part of the world. This is what being born comes down to: it is the proof that we are nothing more than a metamorphosis, a minute modification of an infinitesimal part of the flesh of the world. But the part of our mother's body that we have incorporated into our own – as well as the seemingly smaller part of our father – is only one step in an endless chain of transformations and incorporations: before we became what we are, we were a part of their body, but also a part of what each of those two bodies was before we were conceived. We are connected to an ancestral past, making each of our bodies a limited and infinitesimal part of the history of Earth, the history of the planet, of its sun, of its matter.

All living creatures are, in a certain sense, the same body, the same life and the same self, continually passing from form to form, from subject to subject, from existence to existence. It is this same life that animates the planet, which itself was also born, escaping from a pre-existing body – the Sun – generated by the metamorphosis of its matter 4.5 billion years ago. We are all a piece of it, a spark of light. Energy, solar matter, attempting to live differently from how it lived in its innumerable previous existences. And yet this common origin – or, better, the fact that we are the flesh of the Earth and the light of the Sun discovering a new way of saying 'I' – does not entail that we are simply identical to them. On the contrary, it is because of this deeper and more intimate kinship (we are the Earth and the Sun, we are their body, their life) that we are destined to deny, at every moment, our nature and our identity, and forced to shape new ones. Difference is never a nature; it is a destiny and a task. We have no choice but to become different, we are obliged to metamorphose.

Birth and Nature

Birth is the most individual and individualizing process a living being can experience. Not only is it the threshold of the intimate, it is what makes intimacy possible and defines its boundaries. There is nothing more universal: not only were all women and men present, past, and future born, regardless of gender, class, culture, or orientation, so were all living beings, regardless of species, class, or kingdom. An oak tree, a cat, a fungus, and a bacterium are all beings defined by birth.

Birth is the first of all our experiences, and their transcendental form. But it is also the one we share with every being on this planet, the experience that makes our own self indiscernible from that of other living beings, regardless of their position in the great tree of evolution. It is not a common root, a distant origin that we share. On the contrary, it is the condition of possibility and the form of the continuity of all living beings, all living species, but also of life and its milieu. Birth is a corridor: a transformative channel that leads life from one form to another, from one species to another, from one kingdom to another.

It is in this corridor that individuals, species, and the

planet are able to communicate and metamorphose into one other. Birth renders individuals of the same species indistinguishable, but also makes one species indistinguishable from another, and the totality of all living creatures from the Earth. Our genealogy is therefore always of a cosmic, not just a familial, order. The navel is the mark of our bond not just to our mother's body, but to the Earth and to all living things.

It can happen, as we ourselves have experienced, in a mother's womb. It can happen inside a sphere whose walls are made of calcium. It can take place in the open air or in the ocean, through the union of two unicellular bodies that share a genetic heritage. Or, as with viruses, it can take the form of an occupation and manipulation of the chemical essence of another's body. But one is always born in another body: this is precisely what we call nature. More than just producing a blood tie with parents, to be born is to add a link in the chain of life's transformation. To be born is therefore to *be* nature, and what is called nature is the mode of being of all that is born: everything that exists only through and by virtue of birth is natural. Nature is not synonymous with essence. We natural beings are those who came into the world through this slow process of the migration and appropriation of bodies.

To be born is to be nothing other than a reconfiguration, a metamorphosis, of something other. To be born – to be nature – means having to construct, to build one's own body from the Earth, from all the matter available on this planet of which we are both the modification and the expression, both an articulation and a folding. To be born is to be made of the same material from which all things before us were made.

To be born, for every living being, is to experience being a part of the infinite matter of the world, which in us discovers another way of saying 'I'. We need not study every part of the globe to sense the world, to see it, to experience it in all its infinity. All we need do is explore the material and spiritual memory of our own body. Each of us is the history of the Earth, or a version of it, a possible conclusion.

To be born, for every living being, means not being able to separate one's own history from that of the world, not being able to distinguish between the local and the global. We are born in a specific and irreplaceable body, born of and engendered by another specific and irreplaceable body, but every living creature expresses the life of the entire planet, past, present, and future.

It is always Gaia who says 'I' in us. We are world, and each of us is worldly in our own way. Together we are its content but also, and above all, its form. The 'I' is never a purely personal function or activity: it is a telluric force.

Cosmic Twins

It is births that shape the world. It is only at birth, and only because we are born, that places, air, water, fire, people, memories, dreams, and lies, can come to belong to one another, can become coherent, become flesh. It is only because we are born that there is a world and not just a disparate set of objects. Birth is a double process, both parallel and simultaneous, shared by self and world. For it is not only the living being that is born: the world is also born, and born differently with the appearance of each new individual. Every birth is a twin birth: world and subject are heterozygous twins, born simultaneously, impossible to define apart from one another. Conversely, everything in the world is defined by a relationship of twinhood with everything else.

Birth is not just an event of distinction and separation. It is also a movement of confluence and assimilation into the collective. Every birth is a penetration into a foreign body: its domestication, its habituation. The order of birth simply redistributes the body of the Earth. Because of this order, because of nature, all beings that are born, all living things present, past, and future, have been made, are made, and will be made of the same matter.

The ferns that brush against our feet when we walk in the forest, the poultry we eat, the poplars and plane trees that line the streets of our cities, the insects that irritate us and the microbes in our intestines are all linked by a cosmic consanguinity – Siamese twins that cannot help but utilize and connect to the body of others, or reincarnate themselves in the body of others. In every case, to be born means to take over a body that was the body of another (one's mother, one's father, but also, through them, all the others) and to make it our own flesh. We are never just daughters and sons, just as we are not just brothers and sisters. We share the same face. Which doesn't mean that we have to look alike: trees don't look like us, any more than a microbe or a zebra does. And yet, because we all have birth in common, we draw our life from the same body.

The sharing of this transcendental structure of our being-in-the-world amounts to more than just the necessity of penetrating and appropriating a common body. Above all, it means having a relationship of twinhood with other living beings. Being nature means being a twin of all living things.

Twinhood is not a relationship defined by physical or genetic resemblance. It is the relationship between two or more people who share the same birth – same time, same womb, same mother. They may be genetically different (heterozygous twins); they may not resemble one another at all. But so long as they have shared a womb and have come into the world, so long as they coincide in and through their birth, their existence will be characterized by a commonality that goes deeper than that of form or identity. Seeing all living beings as united by and in birth – seeing them all as natural beings – means seeing them as cosmic twins.

In twinhood, the horizontal relation between twins

transcends the mediation of the parents: it is a far more intense relationship than just having the same parents. This intensity derives from the obvious fact that, in spite of all the physical, material, and formal differences, the continuity of the two bodies is such that any affirmation of self implies an identification with the other. The twin is that being who is exposed to the self-evidence of the contingency of the self and its difference: each twin could have found himself or herself in the body of the other.

Far from being paradoxical and rare, twin births are the very paradigm of birth on a planetary scale. All living beings have one mother, Gaia, whom they share with millions of other beings.

Not only are all beings of the same species twins, all species are twins: humans, ants, oaks, cyanobacteria, and viruses are all just heterozygous twins continually duplicating the reality of the world of which they are the body and mind.

Giving Birth, or the Migration of Life

Everyone forgets that they were born. We live in a culture produced and dominated by those who, by definition, have never had the experience of giving birth to others: males. This is probably why we are so obsessed with death and aging.

Our society is still based on the cult of the dead: we carefully contain their bodies in sealed boxes, we erect mausoleums for them, we continually cultivate their memory. We fill entire library shelves with our reflections on death. Birth, on the other hand, remains a mystery and a taboo. The age-old exclusion of women from the fields of discourse and art has made rare, difficult, and inaudible any expression or sharing of astonishment at the emergence of a new self. Birth is hardly ever honoured collectively. We barely talk about it or celebrate it, we barely pay attention to the way this event marks our bodies and souls.

Everyone forgets. And yet some harbour within their bodies the ability to learn afterwards what being born might mean. For them it is an immediate physical experience. Giving birth to another means reliving one's own birth in reverse: the true antithesis of birth is not death, but seeing one's own body engendering other bodies. Seeing one's body transformed into a matrix through which there passes a life that is no longer personal or individual, since it transits and is transmitted from one individual to another, from one body to another, without negating the individuality and autonomy of either. Seeing one's body doubled, form upon form, organ upon organ, breath upon breath. Seeing one's body transformed into a sea where life migrates from self to self, from individual to individual, from gender to gender.

This second body to which we give birth and which is born autonomously in us, is at the same time a foreign body, an alien and a twin body. It has a different face with unfamiliar features because it is born of the fusion of two faces. Half the time it is of a different gender. And yet it is our body that the newborn baby domesticates and tames: there is not just a morphological analogy, but a physical, material, and spiritual continuity between the two bodies. For nine months, mother and child are coextensive: while remaining two different beings, two subjects (even legally speaking), two lives, their bodies coincide in *res extensa*, occupy the same space, are made up of the same atoms, and are one and the same flesh – a flesh which no longer belongs exclusively to either one of them. It is this continuity – a simultaneous spatial coincidence and autonomy – that is the transcendental form of what is called metamorphosis, and which constitutes the metaphysical mystery of all birth.

The life that animates us is not exclusively ours, it can pass *salva veritate* to a body and an individual who will have nothing (illnesses, tastes, experiences, opinions, death) in common with us. It overflows our bodies, it migrates, it can multiply and detach itself from us like a seed blown away from the tree that gave birth to it and of which it is a part. This life is always ready to go elsewhere, to build other bodies from our bodies. Pregnancy is nothing but the experience of this original multiplicity intrinsic to all life: experiencing one's body as the coextension of at least two subjects, two genera, two life forces that share and draw upon the same life, a life that previously animated the thousands of bodies that engendered us. Our life is never purely singular, unique, indivisible. That is why there is not, and never could be, a form of life as such, a transcendental unity between a life and its form: birth is precisely the negation of any such transcendental synthesis. We always come from another form, we are its deformation, its variation, its anamorphosis.

Conversely, some of the most powerful bodies among us can generate from their own form a different form that shares the life that animates them. Multiplicity is the most profound truth of life. But this multiplicity is not simply arithmetical, and it does not negate the profound unity (material, carnal, and psychic) of all living beings. If there is multiplicity in the living being, it is because life boasts a continuity in transformation: it is impossible to extend oneself indefinitely without undoing one's own form and making one's own life, the most intimate, the most personal, the closest to oneself, inhabit something different. The multiplication of living beings and their variation does not multiply life itself, which is in fact the same for all living beings (otherwise, neither birth nor evolution would be possible).

To experience pregnancy – to experience seeing your own body reborn in the body of another – is also singular for another reason: it belongs to a very particular temporality. With every pregnancy the present finds itself inhabited by the copresence of a prehistoric time that coincides with the origins of a species (for every birth coincides with the birth and creation of the human species), along with an absolute future that lies well beyond the imaginings of science-fiction. Birth is a contraction of time: present, past, and future. It always lies at the threshold between history and that which is irremediably outside it.

Giving birth means undoing history (including one's own personal history), undoing the age of one's body, and undoing the time of present and past so as to construct a kind of artificial, technical, cultural prehistory common to mother and child. A gestating body is a body that constructs a youth that is not purely historical because it does not lie at the beginning of the mother's life, but at an arbitrary moment in it. For an instant, the mother's body becomes something that falls short of either youth or old age, a kind of nucleus of life that germinates in her body. And in this nucleus the mother herself is as if brought back to a time and a mode of being prior to her own birth. This pre-individual, pre-personal nucleus without predefined gender is a laboratory both intimate and universal, a space-time of metamorphosis that alters the mother, the child, the human species, and even the planet. It is not the Earth that incubates and engenders the living, it is the living who, by means of gestation, give birth to the planet, each in their own different way.

Giving birth therefore means allowing the Earth to pass through your body so as to carry it elsewhere. All childbirth is a continuation of plate tectonics, of the movement that allows Gaia to shift her position. From this point of view, birth is a process of migration: giving birth means that life, its force, its self, migrate to another place and into another body. Being a mother (or father) means being able to migrate from body to body, allowing the self that entered us from elsewhere to migrate to other destinies and other life forms. Every self is a migrant, and this divine self can never be identified with any single one of its identities.

That is why motherhood is not an experience limited to one gender. It has no essential link with the feminine: it is birth that makes the mother, and not the other way around. Motherhood is neither a destiny nor an essence nor a gender determination: it is the result of what birth does to certain bodies. This non-essential character of birth is made evident in childbirth. For it takes labour to become a mother, and not only the labour of childbirth. Birth always opens up a space of technics, a place where labour and imagination, force and consciousness, mental effort and physical effort have to join together, and can do so in many different ways. Conversely, we should begin to see what we call 'technics' above all as a variation on what takes place in motherhood. It is because living beings are capable of giving birth – because they can become mothers – that we can manipulate the world, transform it, make the world participate in this metamorphic momentum that we call life. It is birth, the work of mediation between the different forms in which life is embodied, that makes all technical manipulation possible.

Carnival of the Gods

Not enough has been written on birth, and where the subject is broached it tends to be relegated to the margins of 'nobler' subjects. And yet abundant iconographic representations exist and have for centuries fuelled reflection on the phenomenon of birth. Indeed, nativity is one of most common subjects in European painting. But the painter's gaze is distorted by the theological lens. What is depicted is no ordinary birth, but a unique, one-off, unnatural event. Christian theology has contributed to making birth unthinkable by allowing it to be placed outside any naturalistic framework, by opposing birth to nature, by presenting it as a miracle.

In the Christian myth, birth becomes a synonym for absolute novelty, for an experience of a power that completely transcends any natural order whatsoever. Nature in its entirety is taken out of play. As we read in an apocryphal gospel:

> In that hour all became quiet with deep silence and awe. For even winds stopped and gave no breeze, and not a single leaf on trees was stirred nor sound of waters heard; rivers did not flow, nor did the sea wave, and all the gush-

> ing waters grew silent; no human voice made a sound, and there was great silence. For indeed, from that hour on even the heavenly firmament had ceased its rapid course and the measures of hours all but passed away. All things had become silent in a great awe and were stupefied, while we were attending on the coming of the Highness, the end of the ages.[1]

This is a birth detached not only from nature, but also from motherhood: there is a reciprocal dispossession of mother and child here, both physiological and metaphysical. The mother stands before the child in adoration:

> When the light had thus come forth, she adored the one she saw she had borne. And the child was radiating intensely about like the sun, clean and most pleasant to look at, because he appeared alone as peace bringing calm to everything.[2]

This theology of nativity has reduced birth to a purely feminine question: woman has the capacity to bear life without knowledge of the man (*nesciens virum*) and without the male seed (*non ex semen viri*). The labour therefore falls exclusively to woman.

The nativity of the god, the paradigm of all nativity, different from that of others (*verbum caro factum non ut caeteri nascuntur infantes*, in the words of Paschasius Radbertus), is without sin, without pain, free of desire, of any mixedness and any metamorphosis. Little by little this extraordinary event has become secularized and, by extension, has become the model for human birth. The most obvious example of this is to be found in the works of Hannah Arendt who, in contrast to the doctrine of her master, Heidegger, according to whom only man experiences death, saw birth as the human and anthropogenetic experience par excellence:

paraphrasing mediaeval theology, one might say that, according to Arendt, 'Man becomes flesh not as others are born [*homo caro factus non ut caeteri nascuntur viventes*].' Thus, referring to Virgil's *Eclogues*, which she sees as 'a nativity hymn, a song in praise of a child's birth and the arrival of a *nova progenies*, a new generation', Arendt speaks of 'the divinity of birth as such'.[3] Birth is 'the entry of a new creature that appears in the midst of the temporal continuum as something entirely new'. It is in this respect that birth concerns humans above all: only human beings are born, for only they are '*initium*, newcomers and beginners by virtue of birth', and only they 'take initiative, are prompted into action'.[4] It is only with the appearance of humans, according to Arendt, that 'the principle of beginning came into the world'.[5] Only humans can truly be born, for they alone are capable of beginning and of action. And conversely, it is birth that makes us truly aware of the newness that is proper to action: 'Without the fact of birth, we would not even know what novelty is.'[6]

It is not easy to liberate oneself from this two-thousand-year-old legacy. But in order to do so, rather than getting rid of Christian dogma, it might perhaps be necessary to imagine reversing its central intuition, or rather radicalizing it to the limits of the imaginable: fighting fire with fire, countering a bad form of theology with a better one. We would have to imagine then that, if God participates in birth, he must be incarnated in any natural being whatsoever: an ox, an oak tree, an ant, a bacterium, a virus; that if birth brings salvation, it does so with every birth, at any time, in any place. We would then have to think of every birth as simultaneously a kind of divinization, a transmission of the divine substance, but above all as a kind of metamorphosis of the gods. God would then contain within his unity all living beings, and, conversely, each and every living being would be an instance of the multiplication of divinity, in a theological carnival before which all historical religions would pale in comparison.

This perspective was in fact envisioned by Samuel Butler, the famous English writer, author of *Erewhon* and a great reader of Darwin. 'God', Butler writes in his book *God the Known and God the Unknown*, 'cannot become man more especially than He can become other living forms, any more than we can be our eyes more especially than any other of our organs.'[7] In this new economy of incarnation, man cannot and must not occupy a privileged place. 'We cannot admit that one living form is more like God than another':[8] the unity of the living is the mark of divinity. 'It is certain', writes Butler,

> that all living forms, whether animal or vegetable, are in reality one animal; we and the mosses being part of the same vast person in no figurative sense, but with as much bona fide literal truth as when we say that a man's finger-nails and his eyes are part of the same man. It is in this Person that we may see the Body of God – and in the evolution of this Person, the mystery of His Incarnation.[9]

If birth – and metamorphosis – is the force that connects living things to one other in a bond of continuity that is at once biological, genetic, and carnal, then we cannot interpret it, as Butler does, in terms of a personal or organic unity. For such a perspective neglects or represses the point of view of those who give birth. It is no longer the god who gives birth to the world, nor the world that gives birth to a god in human form. Every birth is the process of the migration of gods.

The Speech of the Earth

We are all a repetition of a past life. Since life must constitute itself through birth, it is always a repetition. No origin is possible; life is always a new version of that which preceded it. This is why all questions regarding the origins of life are paradoxical and end up in aporias. As a repetition, each life has an ambiguous relationship with the past, of which it is at once symbol and index: it contains this past within itself and is its embodied expression. Yet in being so expressed, the past is not simply signified in the service of memory or remembrance, it is rearranged, arbitrarily reconstituted, transfigured. For the same reason, all life is of a symbolic nature. This was the case even before the appearance of verbal language: every life, in its body, is already language. It is birth that makes of anatomical and physiological forms something that has the status of a sign.

This observation is central to one of the few theoretical reflections on birth, delivered by one of Freud's most brilliant and heterodox students and friends, Sándor Ferenczi. In an astonishing work, *Thalassa: A Theory of Genitality*, which first appeared in German in 1924, Ferenczi put forward the idea that all life forms consist in 'the repetition of archaic forms of existence' which in this way continually attempt to free themselves from an immemorial trauma.

Birth, according to Ferenczi, is 'nothing but a recapitulation on the part of the individual of the great catastrophe which at the time of the recession of the ocean forced so many animals, and certainly our own animal ancestors, to adapt themselves to a land existence'.[10] In fact,

> [i]n the earliest attempts at coitus on the part of fishes, after the recession of the oceans, it was a matter of attempting to regain in an animal body the moist and nourishment-providing habitation of the sea, now lost. A comparable but even more archaic cataclysm may have forced the unicellular organisms, similarly, to eat each other up, in such manner that no one of the participants in the struggle succeeded in annihilating its opponent. Thus a compromise-like union may then have come about, a kind of *symbiosis*, which after a certain duration of this symbiotic relationship again regressed to the *status quo ante*, in that from the fertilized cell the original germ cells became again differentiated.[11]

Already in Lamarck's writings, the environment and the anatomy of the living are seen as being in a symbiotic relationship: anatomy is always a symbol of the past environment that determined its formation, and, conversely, the environment has been shaped by the beings that lived within it. But with Ferenczi, symbolism acquires a transgenerational quality: every form of life is both the symbol of a catastrophe or trauma and the sign of its overcoming. 'What we call heredity is perhaps, therefore, only the displacing upon posterity of the bulk of the traumatically unpleasurable experiences in question.'[12] Our genetic identity 'represents the sum of the traumatic impressions transmitted from the past and handed on by the individual'; our DNA is a collection of 'engrams', hieroglyphics of all the battles, and especially the defeats, experienced by all those living beings whose will to redemption and salvation we embody. From this point of view therefore, in the symbolism of which every living body is both the language and expression, the one who speaks, the speaking subject, is always the planet itself.

Indeed, according to Ferenczi, there is a 'symbolic identity of the womb with the sea and the earth on the one hand, and of the male member with the child and the fish on the other'.[13] Motherhood is a cosmic fact: 'the mother would, properly, be the symbol of and partial substitute for the sea, and not the other way about'.[14] Not only is motherhood always a geological and planetary function, but the living being itself is the symbol of the entire Earth. In this way, life has enabled the cosmos to express itself.

Metamorphosis as Destiny

Once we are born, we no longer have any choice. Birth makes metamorphosis our destiny. We are in the world only because we are born. And vice versa, being born means that we are a part of this world: we formally and materially coincide with Gaia, with her body, her flesh, her life force. This coincidence involves something stranger and more complex than a simple topological inclusion of the Earth within our body. We are certainly a part of this world, but a part whose shape we had to alter. We are a handful of atoms and bodies all of which were already there, upon which we sought to, were able to, and indeed had to impose a new direction, a new destiny, a new form of life. We are a metamorphosis of this planet, every one of us; and it is only through metamorphosis that we have been able to come into contact with ourselves and all other bodies. We changed the piece of matter that sheltered us so as to enter into the world. We appropriated the bodies and the lives of our parents and modified their course: their DNA, their selves, their smile, their voice, and their accent were all hijacked, inebriated in our body.

Our life began with the act of metamorphosing the life

of the other. This is what being daughters or sons (i.e., being born) means above all: being obliged to become agents of the metamorphosis of others' bodies – our parents', the world's. And this does not end with pregnancy and birth: the metamorphosis is never-ending. The self is always a differential.

We continue to live only by extending this same gesture. The metamorphosis never stops. It is not just a birthmark, it is a destiny. It is not a past event now unavailable to us, it is every living body's mode of life. It does not describe a form of passivity, it is the infinite space of the activity of the living being in relation to itself and to the world.

Metamorphosis is adhesion to and coincidence with another body – the body of another that we adopt, and which gradually domesticates us. Undergoing metamorphosis means being able to say 'I' in the body of the other. Every metamorphic being – every being that is born – is composed and inhabited by this otherness, which can never be erased. Even when we construct something far removed from what we started with (i.e., what is called heredity), the other remains within us. Indeed, the concept of heredity perfectly expresses this aspect of things: what is most intimate and deepest in us, our genetic identity, comes from others, has been concocted by others. We can never say that we 'are' our form, but only that it is something we have, a habitus. We can never integrate it entirely, it always remains a mark of otherness within us. But this otherness has been passed on to us and is now subject to change. Heredity expresses the possibility of appropriating and modifying what once belonged to others.

From this point of view, metamorphosis is the condition that obliges us to nurture the other within ourselves, without ever being able either to be entirely ourselves or to merge or fuse completely with the other. This is what it means to be born: to be impure, to not be ourselves, to have within us something that comes from elsewhere, something foreign that impels us over and over again to become strangers to ourselves. We carry within us our parents, our grandparents, their parents, prehuman apes, fish, bacteria, all the way down to the smallest atoms of carbon, hydrogen, oxygen, nitrogen, etc. We will never be homogeneous, transparent, or perfectly recognizable.

Metamorphosis is not simply the succession of two differences, it is the impossibility of replacing the other, the paradoxical coexistence of the most distant possibilities in one and the same life.

Mirror of the World

Like everyone else, I have forgotten everything. No image comes to mind. We collect images, we store them, we archive them. We hang them on the walls of our rooms, we collect them in our mobile phones, we treat them as a substitute for our faces. We take everything we have seen, heard, felt, and touched to be the truth of the world. Yet we know nothing of what we heard, felt, and saw in the very first moments of our existence, and we do not want to know anything of it. The first image of the world. What we saw and felt when just out of the womb. With eyes still incapable of seeing.

Like everyone else, I have forgotten everything. Or perhaps I haven't forgotten. Perhaps this taste and smell, this light, and these very first images have become the fabric and flesh of all perception. Perhaps it's because of this image that everything seems to be in the world. Perhaps it is this image that makes things into the things, colours, shapes, and realities of this world.

When we think of an image of the cosmos, we think of a photograph, AS17-148-22727, the so-called 'Blue Marble', taken on 7 December 1972 from space, at a distance of around 29,000 kilometres from our world.

Every time we think of the Earth, we think of this sphere lost in the void. Yet we need not leave Earth's orbit and go into space to obtain an image of the planet. Each of us is such an image.

To be born is not just to be a part of the world. It is also and above all to become an open atlas of the world: every living being is not only a world, it is a mirror destined to welcome into itself, as an image, the world itself. We are the world as subject and as image.

Life is not only a transformation of the world: it is the moment when the world is reflected in one of its parts, when it becomes an image caught within one of its parts. What we call consciousness is nothing but this reflection of the Earth upon itself, and every living being is necessarily a consciousness of the world: an image of the world not as anatomy but as mirror. It is not even necessary for it to be perceived as such: every living being simply is nothing but this capacity to reflect the totality of the world in everything it does, to become and to retain within itself the image of the entire planet. We do not need globalization to discover totality: in the heart of every living being there is a perspective on all things. And this perspective, this totality, is not that of an object but that of a possible life. A way of allowing the world to find a home.

Like everyone else, I have forgotten everything. I could not help but forget. Every new life is a new home for the planet, a new way for the planet to say 'I' – and for this to happen, the planet, also, must forget itself. With each birth, in each of us, in each of its living beings, the Earth forgets what it is, or what it was up until that moment, and sculpts its face, constructs its history differently. No matter whether it does so in the body of a maple tree or that of an eagle – for every living thing is the very reincarnation of the Earth.

2

COCOONS

Transformations

I've often dreamt of it. Shutting myself up in a cocoon, it doesn't matter which: a room in my apartment, a country house in some faraway land, a submarine at the bottom of the ocean. Cutting off all relations with the world and giving myself over entirely to the transformative workings of matter. Feeling my soul carving itself out and knitting itself together anew, in a new form. Sensing a force that sculpts it, changing it through and through. Awakening to find nothing of what I thought belonged to me, what was me. Awakening and realizing that even the world around me has been irreversibly altered – in texture, in intensity, in luminosity.

I've often dreamt of it. Shrouding myself in silk until I'm cut off from the world for days on end. Building myself a soft, simple egg inside which I can allow my body to work, going through a change so radical that the world itself will no longer be the same. No longer being able to see in the same way. No longer being able to hear in the same way. No longer being able to live the same way. Becoming unrecognizable. Living in a world that has itself become unrecognizable.

I've often dreamt of it. Wielding the power of the

caterpillar. Seeing wings sprouting from my worm-body. Flying instead of crawling, borne by the air instead of the ground. Going from one existence to another without needing to die and be reborn, in doing so turning the world upside down without even touching it. The most dangerous form of magic. The life that is closest to death. Metamorphosis.

I have long wondered why it was only a dream. Why I never experience it in the waking state. First of all, there is a certain discomfort regarding change.

We have made fetishes of movement and transformation. And yet we do everything possible to make movement impossible. We aspire to move, to change our position in society, to move to a new home, to pass from one state to another. But all of these changes are illusory: we merely move the same life into a new setting – a pleasant trompe-l'oeil that diverts attention from the cobwebs that remain intact on the old furniture of our souls. Globalization promised a mobility unprecedented in the history of humanity, but it has proved to be a global-scale variation on the same old wild-goose chase. There is feverish movement everywhere, but everyone remains as they were. The rich stay rich, and on arrival the poor are still poor, with no more opportunities than they had when they set off. Westerners remain Westerners wherever they are, Africans continue to be excluded and disciplined in the West. If world society or geography is altered by these movements, it is only in so far as they are two sides of the same Rubik's Cube: the nature and number of colours remain the same, only their positions change.

We proclaim our all-consuming love for the transformation of the world, for its progress and improvement, but any real change terrifies us. We advocate the replacement of the objects that surround us, but we secretly hope that this will not alter our identity: we hate to lose all that we are attached to. We have transformed the world to its core and yet this change paralyses us: we hold back from accompanying it with a change in ourselves.

In each case the transformation is only a simulated one. Each time, the movement gets bogged down. Something holds us back, something distances us from metamorphosis.

We usually think about transformation and change according to two models: conversion and revolution. But metamorphosis is neither of these.

In conversion it is only the subject that changes: their opinions, their attitudes, their way of being are transformed, but the world remains, and must remain, the same. Only a world left untouched by conversion can testify to the transformation of the convert. Conversion is often the outcome of an inner journey, full of trials and revelations, long periods of abstinence and asceticism. Such change presupposes absolute and total self-mastery.

Nothing could be further from metamorphosis than a conversion.

Conversion is seductive, in that it exhibits and testifies to the omnipotence of the subject. The convert will be obliged to tell their friends *ego non sum ego*: 'I'm not the same person you once knew.' They will have to repudiate all of their memories and repress their former life or amputate a part of themselves. They will have to take on a new face and a new identity, change their garb along with their morals, and definitively leave behind their past, reduced to ashes in the fire of their will to change. They will always be able to convince themselves that this change comes from them, and from them alone. The new artificial identity, entirely produced by this faceless 'I' hidden within it, is nothing but a daily celebration of this fully controlled power we seek to identify with so as to protect ourselves from all that is happening in the world.

In metamorphosis, the power that passes through us and transforms us is not a conscious and personal act of will. It comes from elsewhere, it is older than the body it shapes, and it operates outside any decision. Above all, there is no movement of repression, no negation of a past or a former identity. On the contrary, a metamorphic being is a being that has renounced all ambition to recognize themselves in one face alone. The life that passes through the caterpillar and the butterfly cannot be reduced to one or the other. It is a life capable of inhabiting and harbouring several forms simultaneously, and which draws its power from this amphibious character.

The second model, revolution, is better known and more widespread. In this case it is the world that changes; the subject, who causes this change and stands surety for the passage from one world to another, cannot themselves be transformed because they are the only witness to the transformation underway. Revolution is the form of change dearest to technology and politics, both of which seem to think of their relationship to the world exclusively in terms of its radical transformation. Technology is the very paradigm of a change that cannot and must not affect the subject: a technical instrument must not itself be altered when it transforms the object it affects – on the contrary, the effectiveness of a technology is gauged entirely by its externality to the changes it causes. This is why all technics is a practice of the exaltation of the technician, the subject of the practice, rather than a real process of improvement of the object to which it is applied. The same could be said of any politics that takes revolution as its horizon and principal objective. For in the dream of a world entirely constituted by a definite act of will there is very little love for matter or for the world, very little interest in change, but only a great deal of narcissism and an attempt to turn reality into a mirror of oneself. Any revolution, in this sense, is far closer to conversion than might be imagined: in both, the subject contemplates their own power.

Revolution is as far removed from metamorphosis as conversion is. For over two centuries now we have thought of technologies as extensions of anatomical organs, in a double sense. In the first sense, the technical object is an out-of-body reproduction of the shape of one of the organs of which our body is composed: the hammer is an imitation of the forearm and fist, glasses an imitation of the crystalline lens of the eye, the computer of the nervous system. In the second sense, all technical objects are supposed to reproduce the subject and their will outside their body, thus making the world into an extension of the self. This is the exact opposite of what happens in metamorphosis. A cocoon is not an instrument for the projection of the self outside the limits of the anatomical body. On the contrary, it involves the construction of a threshold where all borders and identities – of self and world – are temporarily suspended. It is the chiasmus that makes the world into a laboratory of the genesis of the self, and makes the self into the most precious matter in the world, that which continually transforms it.

Insects

They are everywhere. They are innumerable. They have managed to differentiate themselves from one another like no other class of living beings. It is thought that the overwhelming majority (90%) of all animal biodiversity is accounted for by their anatomical dandyism, with an estimated six to ten million species in existence today. But their somatic imagination is not limited to the invention of new species identities. They also have the ability to take on such different bodies in the course of a single individual life that they were long imagined to be magical beings capable of passing from one species to another. It is as if they condense within the formal plurality of a single individual existence the impulse towards the multiplication of forms that exists between species: insects make planetary biodiversity a question of personal virtuosity.

By transforming itself into a butterfly, the caterpillar produces, within its own lifetime and from within itself, a morphological diversity as marked as that which exists between different species. Insects have managed to domesticate within their own way of life the kind of difference to which only interspecies experience gives us access. Indeed, it was in order to define their way of life that biologists adopted the word introduced by Ovid into the Latin language: metamorphosis. The naturalist Thomas Moffet was the first to borrow the term. His work *Insectorum sive minimorum animalium theatrum* had profound repercussions even in modern political philosophy, because it made the social life of insects a model for thinking about the social life of humans. If all politics is the science of diversity, then shouldn't we turn to the confirmed masters of diversification when asking how to live together?

Insects are masters of metamorphosis, but this has not always been the case: they were not 'born' with this talent, they have developed it over time, which makes the achievement even more incredible. The first insects had no wings and did not undergo any transformation. There is nothing natural, original, or spontaneous about this ability.

It's skin that is to blame. Imagine that, instead of your skin, so soft and downy, you had something like a car body or the steel armour of Optimus Prime or R2-D2. Imagine being supported by your skin as you are now by your skeleton; imagine that you depended upon it to protect you, to give you shape and structure. Then shedding your skin would literally be shape-shifting: with a body like this, all growth is metamorphosis. The fiction that allows us to think that our life takes only one form and that changes only concern the size of its silhouette immediately falls away.

From the insect's point of view everything is form, and any change in dimensions means the production of a new form. There is no distinction between quantitative and qualitative change here: all growth is metamorphosis. Their anatomical structure renders visible what is barely perceptible in the bodies of other living beings: that our form is never something we are given once and for all at birth, it is something we continue to construct and dismantle at every moment of our existence. And if birth is the process of the constitution of form, in metamorphosis birth is no longer a punctual event, but a transcendental form of life as such.

This is why, from the sixteenth century onwards, insects became a testbed for understanding the nature of living beings and their relationship to changes in form. On the one hand, the metamorphosis of insects became the paradigm for thinking about the most radical of transformations. Johannes Goedart, for instance, saw in metamorphosis a symbol or allegory of the resurrection of the dead. Having departed their earthly existence, insects grow wings and fly up into the sky. Like resurrected souls, before reaching this 'new and happier life', they must rest for a certain time 'like the dead, without moving, without eating, until they can acquire a new form of life' and a new body.[1]

Metamorphosis is also a process of purification: just as insects leave behind their old bodies and acquire a new way of life, so too must humans shed their old way of life and adopt a new one.

This comparison, a most radical one, might easily be reversed: metamorphosis as a worldly resurrection that takes place every time our body changes in form. This is why Voltaire referred to the 'various metamorphoses with which the earth may be said to be covered' as a representation of metempsychosis and reincarnation:

> our souls [pass] from one body to another [. . .] An almost imperceptible point grows to become a worm, and this worm becomes a butterfly; an acorn changes to an oak; an egg to a bird; water becomes clouds and thunder; wood is

> turned into fire and ashes; in a word, all nature is more or less a metamorphosis.[2]

In contemporary entomology, this resurrection or reincarnation that takes place in one and the same life is seen in a completely different light. In 1958, for example, the celebrated entomologist Carroll M. Williams compared the life of insects to the juxtaposition of two opposite forms that are 'lived as two successive lives': one organism dedicated solely to 'nutrition and the future of the individual', consisting of 'enormous digestive tracts [. . .] hauled around on caterpillar treads', and another dedicated to 'the future of the species', a 'flying machine devoted to sex'. Metamorphosis is just the mechanism that allows two incompatible bodies to belong to the same individual.

In contrast, others tried to conceive of insect metamorphosis as the most banal of transformations. In an effort to find continuity and unity across all forms of transformation, Jan Swammerdam tried to demonstrate that 'it in reality deserves no more admiration, than [. . .] the transformation observable in plants: In the [chrysalis] the little animal is enclosed like the flower in its bud.'[3] 'This change', he continues,

> which has been preposterously called [. . .] by some a death and resurrection, is no more mysterious or surprising, than what happens, when one of the meanest plants, despised and trodden underfoot, gradually swells on every side; and after producing a bud, by bursting the little case containing it, presents an elegant and beautiful flower.[4]

And, against any position that would see a strong formal discontinuity between the different forms acquired by the insect, Swammerdam repeats ad nauseam that the 'Nymph'

> lies hid within the worm, or its skin, in the same manner as the tender and growing flower is wrapped up in its bud; so that as the flower breaks from the surrounding cup, the limbs of the enclosed insect, by the power which swells and shoots them forth, must, in the same manner, at last burst their prison, and make their appearance, which appearance alone constitutes the nature of the Nymph.[5]

Here metamorphosis is simply a movement of revelation, a paroxysmal blossoming of the living being, like the blooming of flowers. But as we shall see, hidden within this comparison there is an even more radical way of thinking about the multiplicity of forms within the living being.

In both cases, looking at insects means describing various strategies for dealing with the most disparate forms within a single life. Their life seems not to be content to express itself in one form alone: the insect is the life of forms, rather than a form of life. The same could be said of worlds. Whether it is a multiplicity of ages, situations, or real anatomical silhouettes, every insect is a parade of worlds. Metamorphosis allows a life to connect several incompatible worlds: the self becomes a synthesis of many universes, rather than the reflection or mirror of what surrounds it. Contemporary biology often explains the coexistence of the two extremely anatomically and physiologically disparate forms of the larva and the adult form via the hypothesis of ecological advantage: adult and child do not live in the same world, they do not cross paths with each other, they do not compete with each other. They embody a life that is not constrained to just one species-world, one ecology, one landscape. The living is always that which combines incompatible and disparate worlds, that migrates from one landscape to another – it is the element that always falls outside ecology.

Every Living Being is a Chimera

The life of insects is a polyptych, and as such is impossible to capture in a single portrait. Several pictures must be combined, one alongside the other. This is why a more precise phenomenology of their life is far easier to achieve via visual or pictorial means than through purely verbal categorization. The canonical classification of the multiplicity of these forms (and their names) was delivered by Linnaeus in his 1767 *Systema Naturae*, where he distinguishes three forms in addition to that of the egg: the *larva*, the *pupa* (nymph or chrysalis), and the *imago*. The three stages already imply a kind of teleology: it is only in the final stage that the true aspect of the insect will be revealed. Modern entomology distinguishes between three cases, speaking of ametabolism when the change appears to be exclusively one of size, as in the Archaeognatha and Zygentoma, and of hemimetabolism or *incomplete metamorphosis* when, as in the Orthoptera, Isoptera, and Hemiptera, the larvae look a great deal like the adults even though they are of different size, have no wings or genitals, and have certain characteristics that are not seen in the adult form. On the other hand, scientists speak of holometabolism or *complete metamorphosis* when, as in the case of the Coleoptera or Lepidoptera (butterflies) among others, the larvae are somatically very different from the adult and an intermediate stage (that of pupation) is present.

And yet it is not easy to orient oneself in this catalogue of phases, of different 'instars' (larval stages) and moments of articulation between one shape and another. It is no coincidence, therefore, that the progress of knowledge regarding metamorphosis was achieved not only through writing, but also through the visual research of one of Europe's greatest illustrators, Maria Sibylla Merian. Born in Frankfurt in 1647, the daughter of the great engraver and publisher Matthäus Merian, she devoted herself from childhood to observing the life of insects, and at the age of thirty-one published her first book devoted to these animals: *The Caterpillars' Marvellous Transformation and Strange Floral Food*. She would later tell of how she was fascinated by the observation of insects from a very early age: 'At the beginning, I started with silk worms in my home town of Frankfurt. I realized that other caterpillars produced beautiful butterflies or moths, and that silkworms did the same. This led me to collect all the caterpillars I could find in order to see how they changed.'[6] It is no coincidence, then, that the first page of her book features the silkworm. Twenty-one years later, in June 1699, she and her youngest daughter undertook a two-month trip to Surinam, where she would remain for twenty-one months studying the local flora and fauna. The results of this research would materialize in her masterpiece, *Metamorphosis insectorum Surinamensium*. In the plates of both books, a graphic and conceptual revolution is at work. In order to depict metamorphosis, she drew a kind of diachronic album that makes a world of the living being itself. The portrait of an insect includes in a single frame 'the origin, food and development of caterpillars, worms, butterflies, moths, flies and other such little animals, including times, places and characteristics'.[7] What before constituted a background now comes to the centre of the image: metamorphosis is the dissemination of a life into the worlds and forms it connects into a unitary framework. It can only be represented as an *open-air atlas* that articulates a series of worlds each populated by a panoply of forms. Every life qua metamorphic force is an atlas in the process of unfolding itself: it does not inhabit a territory, in its very flesh it is the map of the territory. Space is no longer a container for life, instead life itself unfolds many forms and many worlds from out of a single body that in itself embodies a differing, diachronic cartography of the cosmos. Every metamorphosis responds to the obligation of life to make of itself a place, an inhabited space, a territory to be explored and deployed: anatomy and geography coincide.

We might also say that metamorphosis is that which makes it possible to combine a disparate series of worlds and forms into a *single life line*: across these forms a single self expresses itself. Every form, in its most intimate and individual substantiality, seems to be the pure reality of transmission. Therefore, the work of the self is above all that of transmitting one form to another and of transmitting oneself from one body to another, from one world to another. Metamorphosis makes life into a kind of transmission to oneself – a movement that is at once quite close to and opposed to that of pregnancy. Whereas in every pregnancy a single body houses two lives and two worlds, here a single life is distributed between two bodies, between two worlds.

The idea that metamorphosis is the combination within a single life line of two radically different forms and two radically different worlds was expressed in the most radical way by a contemporary British biologist, Donald Irving Williamson. In a series of articles collected in his 2003 monograph *The Origins of Larvae*, Williamson argues that the morphological difference between larvae and adults, in insects as in many marine invertebrates, owes to the fact that 'the basic forms of larvae and embryos were transferred from other taxa and were later additions to the life-histories of existing adult animals'.[8] These are not isolated phenomena: 'Different species occasionally hybridized to produce new animals, which hatched in a form resembling one parent and then metamorphosed into a form resembling the other.' The distance between larva and adult is therefore the distance between two different species: 'the larva and the adult each have their own genomes, and metamorphosis is the change-over from the expression of one genome to the expression of the other.'[9] When 'eggs of one species were fertilized by sperm of another species', there resulted what Williamson calls a 'sequential chimera', 'a hybrid in which the forms of the respective parents are expressed in succession': 'each [. . .] starts its development as a member of one group of animals then metamorphoses to become a member of an entirely different group, frequently of a different phylum'.[10]

This thesis, which has been verified in the case of a few echinoderms, but has not been experimentally confirmed for insects, is in some ways far from surprising. From Merejkowski's hypotheses on the symbiotic genesis of chloroplasts to Ivan Wallin's on the symbiotic origin of mitochondria, by way of Lynn Margulis's research on the widespread importance of symbiotic mechanisms as a fundamental driver of the evolutionary process, biology has accepted a thesis that it has barely yet begun to absorb: if, at the cellular basis of all higher life forms (the eukaryotic cell) there is a symbiogenesis between two individuals belonging to very distant clades (those of bacteria and archaea), then every species is, in its deepest nature, a chimera. All life is of a chimerical nature. What Williamson adds to this intuition is the idea that hybridization played a vital role not only in the early stages of life, but also 'in the later and current evolutionary history of several groups of animals':[11] 'a great many natural animals are really chimeras'.[12] Williamson sets out from the obvious fact that '[n]o larval components or organs contribute directly to adult components or organs'[13] and that '[a] life history that involves dismantling a complex larva then starting again to differentiate an adult'[14] is more difficult to explain via the hypothesis of 'descent with modification' in which 'one body form is replaced by another', than via that of 'metamorphosis by addition' by larval transfer, in which 'the first body form becomes part of the second'.[15] So that, rather than thinking that 'all phases in the life-history of an animal must always have evolved together',[16] we must accept that a life cycle often brings together different evolutionary histories and, conversely, can sequentially express distinct evolutionary outcomes.

Beyond the degree of genetic and morphological commonality, beyond the degree of taxonomic homogeneity, the idea that child and adult do not share the same genealogy is an extremely fruitful one, even for reflections somewhat distanced from strictly biological considerations. Childhood is a kind of reactualized memory of a species, of another life, of a different life – as is adulthood. Our life, even human life which seems to proceed along a morphological and anatomical line far less adventurous than that of insects, is a meeting of forms so disparate that we would need to build cocoons in order to make it possible to pass from one to the other. Metamorphosis exists because all living things find themselves passing, on the same life line, through the most diverse experiences and worlds: it is a corridor that allows the living being not to have to live several lives simultaneously, and allows two lives to cohabit without fusing completely.

A Postnatal Egg

Growth is always the repetition of the mystery of birth. The causes that determine an individual's development are the same as those that determine their birth. For centuries, the metamorphosis of insects has been a privileged site for the astonishment and difficulty of thinking through this obvious fact. Life never entirely leaves the embryonic state, or, vice versa, what we call the embryonic state is in fact a permanent condition: the insect is that form of life for which the egg does not just appear at the beginning, but continues its existence, returns in different forms, as something that follows birth and does not merely precede it. As Carroll Williams said, 'in the metamorphosing insect embryological mechanisms become accessible in a conveniently post-embryonic setting': metamorphosis is simply the transposition of the 'morphogenetic mechanism of the embryo [. . .] into the post-embryonic life of the insect'.[17]

The first to formulate this idea, which modern entomology has long courted, was William Harvey, who coined the term 'vegetative incipience' (*primordium vegetale*) for 'a certain corporeal something having life in potentia; or a certain something existing per se, which is capable of changing into a vegetative form under the agency of an internal principle'.[18] The egg and the seeds of plants are the most common forms of such *primordia*, but Harvey considered the caterpillar to also be a form of this vegetal principle, following in the tradition of Aristotle who first suggested that 'the larva, while it is yet in growth, is a soft egg', and is therefore still imperfect (*De generatione animalium*, 758b):[19] the larva is a kind of egg that has been laid too early, an embryogenetic process that takes place outside the mother's body or, to put it in the words of the great modern entomologist Antonio Berlese, 'a free embryo'.[20] According to Harvey,

> a worm, grub, or caterpillar [is] a kind of mean between a perfect and an imperfect egg, which, in respect of the egg or the primordium itself, is an animal endowed with sense and motion, and nourishing itself; but in respect of a fly, moth, or butterfly, whose primordium it is potentially, it is as a creeping egg, and to be reputed as adequate to its own growth.[21]

The paradox of insect life is that this walking egg, the caterpillar, 'having at length completed its growth is changed into a chrysalis or perfect egg, and ceasing from motion, it is like an egg, an animal potentially'.[22] The chrysalis, the cocoon built by the larva (also known as the pupation stage), is a kind of *postnatal egg*, and the life of insects is therefore that of *an egg that builds other eggs*. As Henson wrote in 1946, metamorphosis is 'the repetition of the developmental cycle which occurs in embryogenesis':[23] insect life is 'a series of repeated developmental cycles all similar in essence to embryogenesis'.[24] According to this hypothesis (today shared by only some of the scientific community), metamorphosis is evidence that it is impossible for any living being to move away from the gestation stage. If it is by birth that we are destined to metamorphosis, metamorphosis also condemns all living things to remain part child: childhood can never leave us, and we will never be able to separate ourselves from it. To change form – to metamorphose – always means having the strength to turn one's body into an egg capable of creating and bearing a new identity. Every self is an egg – and we are a self only because we harbour within us that metamorphic power of which every egg is the expression.

It is as if metamorphosis makes it possible to internalize the capacity for gestation and to apply it not only to the other, but also to one's own life. We are so obsessed with death, decadence, and decay that we no longer realize that every living being is a force of gestation – that every living being gives life to its own forms and to an infinity of others. Metamorphosis is first and foremost this power of all living things to nurture within themselves the capacity to vary the life that animates them. The egg, which insects liberate from its prenatal segregation, bringing it back in the midst of the life cycle, thus becomes the absolute medium, the intermediary between all the forms that life traverses and produces. It is the emblem of the metamorphic state: a state which Harvey describes as 'a mean between the animate and the inanimate world; for neither is it wholly endowed with life, nor is it entirely without vitality'.[25]

The egg, like gestation, is also a hieroglyph in which the relationship between past and future is rewritten. It is, says Harvey, not 'the beginning only, but the fruit and conclusion likewise', 'the mid-passage or transition stage between parents and offspring, between those who are, or were, and those who are about to be'.[26] All metamorphosis – as a perpetuation of the experience of the egg – corresponds to a movement of the contraction of time. Childhood (whether our own, that of the species, of life, or of the Earth) is no longer a prehistoric event; it ceaselessly returns to disrupt the present, forcing it to reformulate itself. On the other hand, thanks to the postnatal egg, the future seems to arrive and deviate the present thanks to a childhood that does not want to consider itself as past. This entails a corresponding change in the image of childhood or youth: childhood is no longer a question of age or lack of experience, it is a question of the relationship between form and act. All life is young in which form remains the object of poetic work, every living being is young that cannot fully recognize itself in the form in which it currently finds itself.

The egg, as work and medium of metamorphosis, also presents us with the paradox of a body the primary purpose of which is to bind the individual indissolubly to its environment. For in every egg the living being encloses itself along with a portion of non-self, a portion of the world upon which it can feed. And in a certain sense this inseparability does not end with the birth of the individual but continues down in the depths, even after the singular event of the cracking of the shell. For the individual, in its connection to the surrounding world, reproduces the structure of the egg. The world itself is an egg that permits the material, structural, and spatial coincidence between living beings and their environment. Ecology ought to be a theory of the egg: every time a living being connects to the space and the life that surrounds it, it does so in order to allow its form to transit outside its body or, conversely, so as to be able to receive within that body the form of what is outside. Every ecological relationship is a metamorphic relationship: the attempt to reconstruct an egg from its milieu.

Conversely, all metamorphosis, qua process of periodic re-emergence of the egg structure after birth, is just evidence that the form of all living things is *the form of the whole world*, and that every living thing is a metamorphosis of the world. The inside flows out into absolute exteriority. For insects, the cocoon is not simply a boundary lying between the individual and its outside – the world, parents, children, the species – but the limit and the space of mediation between the individual and itself, the internal limit of the forms that make up the individual. The cocoon, or postnatal egg, thus marks the threshold where all life makes itself a world and an environment unto itself. Through metamorphosis a body makes of itself a space to be inhabited by forms that are always strangers. The relationship to oneself becomes the perfect equivalent of the relationship between individuals of a species and the relationship between species in the history of life on the planet. Life itself is an egg continually diversifying the form of the Earth.

Rejuvenations

Metamorphosis is a property of bodies that never disconnect from their childhood. Conversely, only a body that is no longer capable of living its childhood – or one which, in anticipation of this, has transferred its childhood to another body by reproducing – will cease to metamorphose. The idea that youth is not just a fleeting stage in the life of a body but a stable and constant structure of any living body has often been embraced in biology. Alexander Braun, one of Ernst Haeckel's teachers, was the first to propose the idea that 'Youth and age are not mere periods of time, into which life may be divided so as to allow us to say, – Youth, ceases here and Age begins',[27] they are organic and spiritual forces that coexist at all times in the life of every individual. Braun continues:

> the phenomena of youth go through life side by side with those of age, in the most varied conditions of exchange, not merely presenting themselves simultaneously in various departments of life, but crowding into the same region, and contending there. Even the child has old teeth, destined to early destruction (the milk-teeth), and young teeth (wisdom teeth) appear even at a late age. Many organs have already

become old and lost their vitality before birth, such as the gills of the Mammalia, the teeth of the whale.[28]

Youth, therefore, is not an age of life: it is a force of rejuvenation (*Verjüngung*) opposite but equal in intensity to the force of aging, and which manifests itself throughout the life of the individual.

The culmination of this radically original vision of the living being is that youth and old age are 'presenting themselves alternately in one and the same course of development; we see youth break forth in age, and enter into the midst of the process, for the purpose of completing or metamorphosing the structures'.[29] Metamorphosis is therefore only the cycle of the various periodic rejuvenations of the living: we are condemned to metamorphose only because we can never separate ourselves from our youth, from the power of rejuvenation that continues to shape our bodies.

Braun sees the plant and insect kingdoms as the places where phenomena of rejuvenation most often appear, but it is a universal phenomenon. 'Without Rejuvenescence', he continues, 'there can be no progressive development; only the lifeless creation, or rather, that dying in the moment of production, the mineral, is devoid of the power of Rejuvenescence; whence it is also deprived of development and propagation.'[30] According to Braun, rejuvenation comes in two forms: an individual return to a previous state of life, and a return to the beginning of evolutionary history as a whole. The first manifests itself as 'Rejuvenescences of the individual within the course of its individual development', while the second achieves a 'Rejuvenescence of the species through the succession of individuals'.[31]

Braun's hypotheses, long regarded as phantasmagorical artefacts of nineteenth-century science, have once again become current following the discovery, some twenty years ago, of an animal capable of reversing its developmental cycle even after sexual reproduction. The organism in question is a jellyfish, known as *Turritopsis dohrii* (or *Turritopsis nutricula*) whose 'transformation potential is unparalleled within the vast array of life-cycle patterns found in cnidarians'.[32] Indeed, the team of scientists including Stefano Piraino, Ferdinando Boero, Brigitte Aeschbach, and Volker Schmid call it 'the first known case of a metazoan being capable of reverting completely to a clonal life stage after having achieved sexual maturity in a solitary stage'.[33] Like the majority of hydrozoans, *Turritopsis* has a life cycle that alternates between a sexual pelagic phase known as the 'medusa' phase, and an asexual benthic phase represented by a colony of polyps. In the latter stage, the animal has a modular organization, which ensures a potentially infinite life span, unlike any non-modular organism, destined for death after sexual reproduction. However, when confronted by environmental adversity or stresses, these jellyfish can regress to their polyp state. The animal, just like the larva in the cocoon, destroys a part of its body so as to take on another form. On the one hand, 'all differentiated somatic cells of the medusa degenerate, and the production of polyp cells is initiated by a set of undifferentiated reserve cells that were not irreversibly committed'.[34] While on the other hand, it would appear that 'differentiated cells of the medusa might transdifferentiate to produce the requisite new cell types': the already differentiated somatic cells change their commitment and gene expression or revert to undifferentiated cells. This transformation, the authors write, 'may be considered a metamorphosis, though in a direction opposite to the usual ontogenetic path'.[35] Normally, in fact, this potential 'metamorphism', which characterizes the early life stages of the medusa, is left behind in the course of development. In this species, though, a true 'ontogeny reversal'[36] may be triggered in response to stress conditions or senescence. The authors comment that the situation is comparable to that of 'a hypothetical insect imago able to reverse to a larval stage after sexual reproduction'.[37]

These jellyfish have apparently radicalized the ability of insects to move nonchalantly from one form to another, and seem to visibly manifest Braun's hypothesis: rejuvenation exists independently of the history and biography of the living being, it is a structural force that animates bodies at all times. All living beings can harden their skin to secrete childhood, can manipulate their bodies, destroy their bones, their flesh, too old and tough to distil a future youth from. The miracle of metamorphosis is this future youth.

Fundamentally, reproduction itself must be seen not as a simple process of multiplication, but as a type of rejuvenation that takes place through the constitution of a numerically different and autonomous body. Indeed, what rejuvenates is always life as such, not the form it takes.

And this is why shape-shifting is often so painful. Metamorphoses are days when everything seems full of violence: the day when the blows we inflict upon ourselves seem harder than any blows the world could deal us. We are closed off, and yet everything hurts. We are locked inside the cocoon to produce childhood. We forget the world and spend hours innocently re-creating the past. What on the outside seems like rejection and violence, on the inside is only creative imagination for an unthinkable and unimaginable future. All living beings hatch and fabricate a future childhood, which belongs not only to them but to the whole Earth.

In fact, the living being itself could be thought of as a process of planetary rejuvenation. As Braun says, 'the ancient changes in the living garment of the earth, appear then as Rejuvenescences of organic nature in mass, and the individual genera and species of the organic kingdoms as subordinate links in its great chain of development'.[38] Life is the Earth's attempt to forget its own nature and history, to forget the body and the memory of the past, in a future that is something more than the logical and historical consequence of what has been. The history of life on Earth is the attempt to rejuvenate the planet – the destruction of its geological identity.

A New Idea of Technics

A cocoon is a postnatal egg which, we might say, is *fabricated* by the individual. It defines a sphere within which being and doing fuse into a third dimension. Above all, this obvious fact defines a characteristic of the phenomenon of metamorphosis that we have so far neglected: its purely technical nature. In all metamorphosis, the living being has to construct its own form, which is therefore not at all natural or spontaneous. As a result of this, the very nature of technics is profoundly transformed.

We usually understand technics as a consequence of the individual's biological shortcomings. Ever since Plato and his myth of Prometheus and Epimetheus, we have got used to thinking of technics not only as a purely human trait, but also as something that corresponds to a lack of biological development. If humans need technics, it is because their bodies are characterized by a biological and natural deficit of power and form in relation to other living beings. The myth tells of how Epimetheus, charged with providing all living creatures with suitable faculties, ran out of powers, having distributed them to all the other animals, thus leaving man 'completely unequipped', 'naked, unshod, unbedded, and unarmed'.[39] This is how Prometheus ended up stealing fire from Vulcan and Minerva, and endowing mankind with technics. Alone among animals, humans possess the art of 'articulating speech and words'; they alone 'invented houses, clothes, shoes, and blankets, and were nourished by food from the earth'.[40]

In contrast to the story that this myth stages, in metamorphosis, technics becomes what allows every body to free itself from its development and to make this original indeterminacy not a problem to be solved, but the form of the global relationship of every living being to itself. Technics serves to dissolve our particularity, to return us to an earlier stage of development, to undo both individual and evolutionary history: it is a fountain of youth, a procedure of rejuvenation. Every technical object is an egg that steals youth from the world and implants it into our lives. We build technical objects in order to produce a shared childhood. And what is rejuvenative in them is always life, not the form that carries it into our bodies. Rejuvenation is always impersonal.

The cocoon as technical postnatal egg thus overturns the modern idea of technics as *Organsprojektion* developed by Ernst Kapp in the first modern book on the nature of technology, published in 1877 in Germany. According to Kapp, any technical object, any instrument, is merely the projection of an organic structure outside the body, in a perfectly isomorphic relationship. The extension of the organ, its projection out of the anatomical body, makes it possible to correct its defects (profoundly strengthening a human body that is so badly equipped compared to that of the other animals) but above all to humanize the world. Thanks to the organ-projection, thanks to technics, the world becomes an extension of the human body. McLuhan's thesis on media as extensions of man is only a further gloss on this theory of Kapp's. From this perspective, technics, firstly, is something purely human (animals and other living beings cannot have technology), and secondly, is something that transforms whatever it affects into something human. The technical world anthropizes everything it touches. This 'extraflexion' of the anatomical form allows man to shape the world in his own image or likeness. In a sense, the same idea is implicit in the concept of the Anthropocene, where once again the technical development of humanity 'humanizes' the cosmos.

In the idea of technics embodied by the cocoon, on the contrary, the manipulation of the world becomes something that allows us to cast off of our own nature, to change it from within rather than to project it outward. Technics – the cocoon – is the relation that every living being maintains with itself and which leads it to radically modify its body and its identity. Any relationship with oneself is therefore technical in nature, its aim being to modify one's own form. Every relationship with oneself produces an egg, a postnatal cocoon, which makes the world into a space for rebirth and self-shaping. We should learn to see in every technical object a cocoon that enables this transmutation: a computer, a telephone, a hammer, or a bottle are not just extensions of the human body. On the contrary, they are ways of manipulating the world that render possible a change of personal identity, ethologically if not anatomically. Even a book is a cocoon that makes it possible to reformulate one's own mind.

Technics – the art of building cocoons – makes of the self at once the subject, the object, and the means of the act of transformation. It is not a force that opposes life or extends it outward, it is nothing but the most intimate expression of life, its original dynamism.

The Metamorphosis of Plants

Metamorphosis is not just a process that affects the overall shape of the body: it is also the relationship that is established between the different parts of the body, allowing each of them to follow a life line, to expand throughout the course of its development. It is also the principle of the equivalence of parts within the same body: in fact our whole body is the result of the metamorphosis of an extremely small piece of matter which had to produce, step by step, stage by stage, the various forms into which it would end up unfolding. Metamorphosis is therefore not just a historical process that divides up the constitution of the living being into a series of differentiated stages. It is above all the synchronic link that makes a body composed of the most disparate forms and functions into something unitary that has travelled one and the same life line. It is by focusing on the life of plants rather than that of insects that biology became conscious of this aspect of metamorphosis. And most of what is today called 'developmental biology' was established in the context of this reflection on metamorphosis as a plastic force inherent in every plant body.

It was flowers that first suggested the idea that at the basis of every vegetable being there is an inexhaustible metamorphic nucleus. This was first of all a matter of anatomy: the flower seemed to have a body capable of passing from one form to another without ever being fully determined, as if it were the most powerful and perfect expression of the metamorphic capacity of living beings. As Goethe said,

> nature produces one part through another, creating a great variety of forms through the modification of a single organ. [. . .] Researchers have been generally aware for some time that there is a hidden relationship among various external parts of the plant that develop one after the other and, as it were, one out of the other (for example, leaves, calyx, corolla, and stamens); they have even investigated the details. The process by which one and the same organ appears in a variety of forms has been called *the metamorphosis of plants*.[41]

It was Carl Linnaeus who first noticed this: 'The origin of the *flowers* and the *leaves* is the same.' It is this original equivalence between the flower and the leaf which implies that every organ in the plant is interchangeable with every other. In fact, it is also the case that

> the origin of the *buds* and the *flowers* is the same. A bud consists of the rudiments of leaves. *Stipules* are appendages of the leaves. A *perianth* is made out the rudiments of leaves, fused together. If nourishment is channelled to the scales of a catkin, the florets are destroyed and the scales turn into *leaves. Luxuriant vegetation* produces leaves by continuing after the flowers. *Meagre vegetation* produces flowers at the ending, after the leaves.[42]

The flower is just the most visible evidence that, in the plant, every part is equivalent to every other part. In this respect the animal body cannot hope to imitate the plant body. Whereas in the latter any part can derive from any other, in the former '[t]he parts differ so much that it is impossible to recreate one part from another, or to say that one part is another part in amended form'.[43] As the naturalist Caspar Friedrich Wolff, one of the founding fathers of modern embryology, put it,

> one could not possibly claim or imagine that the liver is a modified form of the oesophagus. [. . .] It is impossible to see in animals what we see in plants: [. . .] that all parts of the body are produced by one and the same generative principle, modified in different ways.[44]

The animal body 'is produced almost by the association of different causes that are not necessarily related or dependent upon one another',[45] whereas the plant body springs from just one generative principle, being the fluid transformation of one part into another. The flower is the proof and manifestation of a principle of absolute anatomical and somatic plasticity: to have a body no longer means to exist in one form, but to have the power to translate any one form into another.

As a consequence of this profound unity, it becomes impossible to separate reproduction from growth: the flower, as emblem of the equivalence and translatability of all anatomical parts of the body, yields an identity between vegetation and multiplication. 'If we consider the plant in terms of how it expresses its vitality', wrote Goethe, inspired by Wolff, 'we will discover that this occurs in two ways: first through growth (production of stem and leaves); and secondly, through reproduction (culminating in the formation of flower and fruit).' The affirmation of the identity of the leaf and the flower coincides with the affirmation of an identity between vegetation and reproduction. Goethe continues:

> If we examine this growth more closely, we will find that as the plant continues from node to node, growing vegetatively from leaf to leaf, a kind of reproduction also takes place, but a reproduction unlike that of flower and fruit; whereas the latter occurs all at once, the former is successive and appears as a sequence of individual developments. The power shown in gradual vegetative growth is closely related to the power suddenly displayed in major reproduction.[46]

Vegetation, then, is nothing but 'successive reproduction', and fruiting is 'simultaneous reproduction'. The blossoming plant 'shows a contraction of all its parts; the dimensions of length and breadth are canceled out, as it were; all its organs develop in a highly concentrated state and lie next to one another'.[47] It is not simply an allegory of the identity between plant and metamorphosis: it is above all an absolute condensation of the plant and the vegetal being.

Long before Goethe, this idea had been put forward by one of Linnaeus's greatest pupils, the one who put him in contact with Jean-Jacques Rousseau: Nils Ericsson Dahlberg. According to Dahlberg, plants are subject to the same type of metamorphosis as insects: 'The metamorphosis of insects consists in the elimination of the armour which then allows the insects to manifest themselves in their perfect naked form', and something absolutely identical happens in plants:

> The bark of plants behaves in the same way as the exoskeleton of insects, which, once shed, leaves the insect naked. This is what also happens in plants when they produce flowers, open and cast off their bark, from which the calyx develops: it is then that we see the inner plant burst out, the flower, while its corolla shines, its stamen impregnated by pollen anthers.[48]

Drawing on Jan Swammerdam's research, Dahlberg acknowledges that 'the metamorphosis of insects is not a true transubstantiation, as Ovid imagined, but only a decortication'.[49] Swammerdam, as we have already seen, had in fact claimed that the larva of the cabbage moth (*Pieris brassicae*), when it is still in the ground, exhibits 'the legs, wings, horns, and other parts of an insect [. . .] under its skin'.[50] Dahlberg concludes that plant metamorphosis is only a 'denudation of parts': 'If we look at the flowers, we see that they are only the plant stripped bare. And if we observe the substance from the stalk to the flowers, we can see that the latter are identical to the stalk and are only a denudation of its parts.'[51] The flower is the plant stripped bare, its purest manifestation.

Goethe later corrected Dahlberg on this 'most interesting parallel between the metamorphosis of insects and that of plants'.[52] It is not a question of thinking of the flower as a simplification via subtraction of the plant body. On the contrary, a flower is a complication of all forms of plant life, their simultaneous co-presence. Indeed, if we compare the metamorphosis of flowers with that of insects, we cannot fail to notice that,

> in the plant, we observe successive states coexisting in the same being; when the flower develops, the stem and the root still exist; fertilization takes place while the preexisting preparatory organs are still full of life and vigour [. . .] In the insect, it is quite different. The insect abandons one after the other the various envelopes that it sheds, and a new being escapes from each one. Each successive state is separate from the former state, and it is impossible to step backwards.[53]

Every flower is the instantaneous recapitulation of the history of an individual plant: the expression of its entire past, but above all the anticipation of its future. In the plant, metamorphosis is expressed with a magnitude and power unknown in insect development. The living being itself seems to become an absolute cocoon.

The Cocoon of the World

The cocoon is the paradigm not only of technics, but of being-in-the-world in general. Insects – those masters of the cocoon, the great demiurges of transformation – have fooled us into believing that the cocoon is a specific, fleeting, ephemeral instrument that plays a role in the lives of certain individuals. On the contrary, it ought to be considered as the transcendental form of all living beings. Wherever a living being relates to itself, to other living beings, and to the planet, there are cocoons. Every self is a cocoon.

First and foremost, a cocoon is proof that our lives cannot be attributed to a single anatomical identity. In the cocoon, life is situated between two bodies, between two faces, between two apparently incompatible identities. The cocoon is the construction of the compossibility of these identities. It is proof that the individual does not live by exclusion, but by the multiplication of faces and bodies.

The cocoon is also proof that our life can never be seen as belonging to a single environment, a single niche, a single world. And this is not because life is capable of adapting to different environments, to different worlds.

It cannot be reduced to a specific world because it is always a world for itself. The cocoon is proof that life builds its entire world; proof that there is no difference between home and world, not because the world is our home but in the sense that life constantly transforms the space in which it unfolds and that, for this very reason, life always inhabits itself.

The cocoon is living proof that an environment, a world, is not just a geometry that must be adapted to, but a laboratory in which, from the very outset, geometry and form are constantly redesigned.

The cocoon is the form and paradigm of self-consciousness: the relationship of the living being to itself is therefore no longer a matter of recognition. Self-consciousness is no longer a site for the living being to discover itself, recognize its own face and coincide with itself. It is the space in which each one of us is subjected to forces that irremediably transform us and transpose us into a world totally different from the one in which we have formerly lived. Ideas, opinions, sensations – whether they come from outside or from our own bodies – are forces that transform us: wings that emerge from our worm-bodies, intercessors of a world that we can no longer roam, that we can only perceive through flight.

The cocoon is proof that metamorphosis is above all the relationship we have with ourselves. And not just on an individual level. Our individual form, whether human being, butterfly or monkey, bacterium or prickly pear, lobster or oak, is a cocoon. This is the deepest meaning of Darwin's theory of evolution. Every life form is a cocoon: the continuous gestation of a metamorphosis the result of which will only reveal itself in the future.

It is a cocoon because no species requires the help of any other in order to construct new forms: it closes in on itself, dismantles its history, destroys and recreates its body, its genes, making a collage, a do-it-yourself reconstruction using what it has at its disposal.

It is a cocoon because the form to which it will give birth can never be either conversion or revolution. It involves no abolition or rejection of the form that preceded it.

Every species, so it seems, is somewhat dissatisfied with its form. Every species wants to break out, to be done with its identity and to build new ones. However, no species ever seems to be able to completely escape the forms that preceded it.

The life of species on the planet is a constant metamorphosis. Metamorphosis is the boundary that separates and divides species from one another. This means that the relationship we have with different life forms is always metamorphic: we could become, we could have become, other. Metamorphosis is the kinship that simultaneously connects and divides all living beings.

We don't need sex or genetic mutation to experience this interspecies metamorphosis. We experience it every day. Many times in a day. Every time we eat, we make ourselves animals. Meaning that for us, living coincides with having to ingest the bodies of other living beings. For us, living coincides with the task of having to assimilate the lives of others, the bodies of others, into our own bodies and lives.

But we don't even need to eat in order to experience being cocoons. It is enough to just begin living. All too often we forget that everything on Earth, everything we see, is a transformation, a metamorphosis of Gaia's body, a variation on the theme of her flesh, an alchemical modification of her life force. We are a metamorphosis of terrestrial rock, its living variant. Everything comes from the Earth – not in the nihilistic or Christian sense in which the earthly is seen as devoid of value, but in the sense that the Earth is a huge cocoon within which all forms are generated. And vice versa, what we call life, in all its forms, is just a cocoon in which Gaia invents a new way of being.

It is the Earth (and therefore the universe, because the Earth is only matter that has escaped from the Sun) that invents in us a new way of being, out of its own matter.

From this point of view each of us, as a cocoon, has lived through everything. We are one world and one substance. The gaps in our self-consciousness and memory are just that: the emergence of other 'selves' in our mind.

Metamorphosis is both the proof that there is only one substance, the scar that connects us to it and to all of its parts (birth connects us to the bodies of others, those of the mother and father whose metamorphoses we are, to sex, food, etc.), and the process of fabricating, constructing, secreting this common substance . . . It is not a soil, a substrate, a ground. It is above all a future, an omnipresent possibility, a virtual reality. And everything leads back to it – especially death. The question is always how to stay oneself for a while, just a little while, how not to destroy oneself.

The world is a cocoon made entirely of cocoons.

Cocoons are everywhere. Every living cell is one. Every individual is one: each one of us is a space within which the world seeks and finds a new face. Cocoons are everywhere. Every environment is one. Every species is one: a life form is the site of a continual metamorphosis that exposes the present to the perpetual erosion of a faceless future. Cocoons are everywhere. The atmosphere is the largest cocoon on this planet. And the Earth, as a whole, is just one huge cocoon that prevents any one subject from becoming too complacent in its power.

Cocoons are everywhere. They do not await the call to conversion or revolution. Inside them there is constructed an unrecognizable and unpredictable future that has already obliged each of us, and everything around us, to change anatomy many times over.

I've often dreamt of becoming a part of it. All around me, just white, soft silk.

I've often dreamt of it. No need to protest. No need to rise up against anyone. No need to putrefy yourself. Just change your skin. Just change your face. Change your body. Become another.

I've often dreamt of it. Not needing to invent a different world. Not needing to reform the world. Waking up and living in a world that has nothing in common with what we know.

This dream is the life of our planet. This dream is the history of life.

3

REINCARNATIONS

Eating and Metamorphosis

For most of us, it happens at least three times a day, yet we hardly take any notice of it. Whether it's plants, animals, or fungi, every day we are used to sitting down and using our mouths and hands to literally incorporate the bodies of other living things: taking their lives, taking their bones and their flesh, and transforming them into our own lives, bones, and flesh. Eating is our name for this strange operation, which is more like an alchemical mystery than a physiological necessity. Very often we tend to see in this operation something embarrassing, humbling, a biological need to be fulfilled as efficiently as possible. Very often we try to conceal what is at stake here, and turn this experience of taking the life of another, something different from us, into a more elevated aesthetic experience, all flavours, smells, and abstract colours. We no longer put a lamb, a tomato, or a strawberry on the table, but abstract qualities of taste, colour, and tactile matter: the idea of acid, astringent, sweet, salty, liquid, solid, yellow, green, brown, or red.

This desire to relieve ourselves of the concreteness of the encounter that takes place every time we sit at the dining table, every time we eat a sandwich or drink wine, every time we go to a restaurant or enjoy an ice cream, is not just a symptom of a desire to ennoble matter or a sign of our spirituality. It is above all linked to a powerful guilt that binds us to food, to our inability to really understand what is involved in eating. This deep sense of guilt is expressed in the debate around vegetarianism: we feel so guilty about the fact that our lives involve the death of other living beings that we prefer to establish an arbitrary limit, an artificial boundary between living beings that suffer (animals) and those that do not (plants). We feel so guilty about this common, banal, everyday, yet miraculous and incomprehensible act that we tend to reduce it to a simple exchange of energy that can be described in terms of pure thermodynamics. For example, there are at least two absolutely extraordinary facts about food that we tend to forget.

The first is that, for us, as animals, as heterotrophic living beings, eating always implies an encounter with other living beings, and being obliged to live off the lives of others. Life feeds on life. A life is never self-sufficient. It doesn't just need more energy (otherwise we could simply plug ourselves into an electrical outlet). It needs to absorb another form of active life into itself, a life that has been constructed by others. Eating does not mean injecting matter into our bodies, swallowing elements and energy. Eating means transfusing the life of others into our bodies. No matter whether they are dead, cooked, smoked, or dried, we need living bodies: what we eat is always and only life. To eat is to merge two lives into one.

We would be wrong to see this necessity as implying negativity and death. It is a misrepresentation to see the act of eating only as a form of sacrifice and violence. This is only a half-truth. Of course, one of the two living beings seems to disappear in the process. But what we miss, what we do not consider when we reduce the act of eating to a mere exchange of energy, is the capacity of each living body to impart life not only to itself but to other living beings. A chicken, a cow, a tomato, a potato, a grain of barley are not only life forms confined within the limits of their bodies: they are bodies capable of transmitting their life by entering the body of another.

In other words, there is nothing individual or specific about the life that animates them: it may remain in their bodies, but it may also come out of them to feed individuals from an infinite variety of other species. There's something extremely enigmatic about this fact. What eating tells us is that the life that each of us seems to consider as absolutely personal and proper to us is in fact essentially anonymous, universal, and capable of animating any type of living body. In a certain sense, every act of eating shows that we have a life that is essentially identical to what we eat. This is demonstrated by the fact that when we die, we will necessarily become a feast for other living beings.

It is both disturbing and startling to realize that the life that lies within the most intimate depths of the being we eat engendered us: that it is exactly the same life that is within us. And this is what eating is above all: the contemplation of this self-same life that, at the same time and by way of the same principle, animates ourselves and the bodies we eat, the contemplation of this life that can live everywhere, inside and outside us. Our body and the body of a goose, a chicken, an apple, a kiwi are all variations of life, an indeterminate life.

Food is the contemplation of life in its most terrifying universality: this life that digests and absorbs everything, that sustains everything and destroys everything, seemingly never content with the form in which it has been received. It seems to have no limit. Indeterminate and omnivorous, it is reluctant to renounce the possibility of further change. Open and indecisive, it is incapable of renouncing any potential future form: a chicken becomes a human being, a human being becomes a worm, a worm becomes a pigeon, etc. There is no closed circle of life. Life goes from body to body, from species to species, never entirely satisfied with the form in which it is found. And that is all eating is: proof that there is only one life, common to all living beings, capable of circulating between bodies and between species. Proof that no barrier of nature, species, or personality can enclose it eternally in one single form, one single species, one single body.

This circulation is both similar to and distinct from the metamorphosis of the caterpillar. For here the same life is distributed between two different bodies, two different selves, without our being able to say which is the caterpillar and which the butterfly.

From this point of view, what we call death is only a metamorphic threshold. Every living being is a cocoon by means of which life builds something different. The fact that for every living person death is only one moment, one aspect of the feeding process of other individuals, shows that in nature nothing dies, everything is transformed: the same common life undergoes transformation and circulates from individual to individual. Each time we ingest a living being, whether plant or animal, we are simultaneously the place, subject, and object of metamorphosis. Every time we eat, we are transformed into a cocoon within which another life form (a chicken, a turkey, a pig, an apple, an asparagus, a lobster) becomes human. Every time we eat, we are transformed into a cocoon within which a human being takes the flesh and life of a cow, a peach, a cod, a caper, an almond.

But there is another, extremely mysterious aspect lurking beneath this banal and obvious activity of eating: in nature, it almost exclusively involves individuals of different species. Eating is always a multispecies encounter. Precisely because life can never be contained in a single form – personal or specific – it must regularly change its face, change its life. In the act of eating, all species encounter one another and must do so. Eating is the most universal multispecies encounter in the world. Far more than through their genealogical links, it is through their eating of one another that the different species produce a world made of the same flesh, something unitary and interdependent. It is by eating (i.e. by infringing their own boundaries) that species constitute a universal community: a community of communities beyond their differences in nature, habitat, and form of life.

Again, eating cannot be seen as the consequence of a simply negative state of being (the fact that someone lacks the substance or capacity to ensure their own survival): it represents the need to encounter the other, to become other, through the life of other species. Eating makes the relationship to oneself into a political relationship: to stay alive one must cross the limits of one's own body and allow a member of another species to cross those limits too. In this sense, the act of eating brings together, beyond borders, all individuals and species that exist in the world. Far from being the hallmark of individual or specific vulnerability, eating is the most radical political act possible. For in this act the nature, form, and existence of borders – in their most biological and metaphysical reality – are at once challenged and mutually renegotiated.

Eating, as the transcendental form and matter of all interspecies interrelationships, therefore has a far broader, more originary and radical meaning than one of fellowship or simple cohabitation. Since Darwin, biological science has accepted that there is a (more or less distant) genetic relationship between all living beings. Living beings have a common origin: reproduction is the site where all species have woven a reciprocal relationship, and it is precisely from this interconnection that life is generated and conceived. Yet the genealogical relationship between individuals and species, which places individuals into a domestic assemblage, is perpetually undone in the act of eating. Eating should no longer be seen as the consequence of biological negativity, but as nature's invitation to each individual to move home, to migrate, to transmigrate from body to body, from place to place, from flesh to flesh. The politics of Gaia is nothing but this daily construction of a flesh common to all living beings, which all of them draw upon, but which circulates not only from place to place but from body to body, from individual to individual, from species to species.

This politics, which in the religious language of European and Asian antiquity was called transmigration, metempsychosis, or reincarnation, is radically anti-domestic in a twofold sense. First of all, because of this migration, life cannot be conceived of as a simple relation of habitation of space. The world is not our dwelling-place: it is the reservoir of our past and future flesh, the archive and virtual catalogue of the lives and identities we had before becoming human and what we are today. Secondly, one's relationship to oneself is not, cannot be, and never will be one of dwelling. The fact that we are obliged to eat, and to eat the bodies of other species, means that living beings cannot limit themselves to cohabiting with (or alongside) one other. No species can limit itself to inhabiting its own body alone. It is obliged to enter the carnal house of the other, to occupy it, to be integrated into it, to become the body of the other, the flesh of other species. We continually migrate, transmigrate, or, conversely (if we are eaten by others) become the home of other individuals and other species. We can never stay home alone. We can never regard the body of the other as their exclusive home. We are obliged to move, to move house, to change our body, or, conversely, to become the house of the other, to make our flesh the home not only of another body, but also and above all of another species. The destiny of all living beings is to become the body of another species, in the same sense that, because of reproduction, the destiny of any species, at least virtually, has always been to betray its own species and to disallow it any form of eternity. Eating is proof of the not just spatial but also metaphysical instability of living beings: living beings never remain what they are, but are destined to move into another species not only through evolution but also through the process of nutrition. The reincarnation that takes place in every act of eating makes the relationship between living beings metastable. Eating is proof that life is infinitely malleable and capable of anything, that the body of life and of living beings can never be enclosed in a domestic and proprietary logic: it is nothing if not the infinite transmigration of matter. We possess nothing, not even our body or our identity. No one is ever at home, especially not in their own body. This is what eating teaches us. No one on Earth *has* a home: not only do we not have possessions, things that belong to us by nature or by genealogy, everything must also be negotiated, made and remade over and over again. No one on Earth lives in their body as in their house; the relationship to oneself is never natural, spontaneous, or definitive. We are constantly moving home, constantly taking over the lives and bodies of others. We ceaselessly become the house and the body of others. No one is ever totally at home. No one in this world follows house rules.

Being Eaten

Now we come to the most disturbing form of metamorphosis. Eating is evidence that it is impossible to consider the form that informs the living being – in its individual and specific identity – as something substantial, autonomous, and above all essential, inherent in the life that passes through it. Through the act of eating, a life can migrate from one form to another or, conversely, can take on opposing forms. On the other hand, through the act of eating all life demonstrates its *physiologically* multispecies and interspecies nature: its need to move from one species to another, from one form to another, as well as its need to take on several forms. Eating thus constitutes the evidence and the reality of a perpetual motion that allows all species at once to construct one and the same life (because eating means discovering some formula for the physiological equivalence between two life forms), but also to constantly differentiate this same life (because eating means transforming one form into another). The repetition of this daily act reminds us that there can be no life on the planet without metamorphosis, and that metamorphosis is the most elementary metabolic process of every living thing, rather than a rare and isolated event to be found only in a few organic cabinets of curiosity.

Feeding – the most common and repeated form of metamorphosis – is also evidence that death cannot be understood as the opposite of life: it is the passage of that life common to all from one form into another. Death can never interrupt life, but only ever changes its mode of existence. A 'corpse' is the life and the food of other living beings. All death is a continuation of life with a new face. And inversely, life is always constituted in the form of a reincarnation of the life that preceded it. Bodies do not describe the ontological limits of that which animates them, but only the boundaries of its temporary manifestation.

It is through its reflection on nutrition that contemporary ecological thinking has come to conclusions of this kind. The most radical of these conclusions come from one of the most sincere thinkers of the last century, Val Plumwood. Her thinking takes as its starting point an experience she had in a canoe on the East Alligator River in Kakadu National Park, Australia. Plumwood tells of how, attacked by a crocodile, she was not afraid of death. She was, however, gripped by a sense of unreality: what was happening was not true, 'it was an illusion! It was not only unjust but unreal!'[1] Our usual cherished image of the world does not include 'the humbling experience of becoming food for another animal', which 'is now utterly foreign, almost unthinkable';[2] it is a world where humans cannot become food 'for sharks, lions, tigers, bears and crocodiles, food for crows, snakes, vultures, pigs, rats and goannas, and for a huge variety of smaller creatures and micro-organisms'.[3] Plumwood felt not only disbelief, but above all *moral* indignation: 'The creature was breaking the rules, was totally mistaken, utterly wrong to think I could be reduced to food. As a human being, I was so *much more than food*. It was a denial of, an insult to all I was to reduce me to food.'[4] This disbelief, as she explains, was not only existential but ethical.

Plumwood devoted a substantial part of her intellectual life to understanding the reason behind this sense of illusion and indignation in the face of the self-evident and trivial physical fact that 'all ecologically embodied beings exist as food for some other beings'.[5] The question is: 'Why was being food such a shock? What kind of shock was it?'[6] In other words, why, despite what we have learned from Darwin, does 'being food [confront] one very starkly with the realities of embodiment, with our inclusion in the animal order as food, as flesh, our kinship with those we eat, with being part of the feast and not just some sort of spectator of it, like a disembodied eye filming somebody else's feast'?[7] Why does the awareness that '[w]e are the feast' for other animals translate into a 'humbling and very disruptive experience'?[8]

Plumwood believes that the ecological crisis we are undergoing can only be overcome if we can manage to accept 'equality and reciprocity in the food web': 'All living creatures', she writes, 'are food, and much more than food',[9] and 'thinking of ourselves as of use as food for others is the most basic way' to think of life as a 'circulation, as a gift from a community of ancestors' – and death 'as recycling, a flowing on into an ecological and ancestral community of origins'.[10]

To achieve this we must free ourselves of the myth that makes us think of ourselves as radically different from everything around us. This refusal to recognize that our life is the same life that passes through any other body is not just a theoretical matter: the claim to be 'different and superior to other creatures', to be made of 'mental matter', has not only driven us to threaten the real extinction of all the great predators and to transform predation into 'something we do to others, the inferior ones, but which is never done to us'.[11] Above all, it has led us to repeat ad infinitum the illusion of superiority and apartheid.

We might then understand the choice of burial in a solid coffin as expressing the need to prevent 'the Western human body (at least sufficiently affluent ones) from becoming food for other species'.[12] Even cremation seems to comfort us in the illusion that our bodies will remain untouchable, when in fact, even in this case, they will eventually end up as food for others – primarily trees that will sequester the carbon released from our bodies. We cannot avoid becoming other living beings.

Here, death becomes a pretext for subtracting our body from the cycle of reciprocity that all terrestrial existence presupposes. As if, even at the point of death, we imagined that our humanity was enough to separate us from the fact that we are nothing more than a metamorphosis of the flesh and life of other living beings, necessarily destined to metamorphose into yet other forms of life. The general cultural tendency is to continue 'guarding ourselves jealously and keeping ourselves apart, refusing even to conceptualise ourselves as edible, and resisting giving something back, even to the worms and the land that nurtured us'.[13]

Reincarnation and the Transmigration of the Self

It is no coincidence that this resistance is most apparent in our conception of and relation to death. In the way we imagine and talk about death we dogmatically posit that the limits of the animation of our body are the very limits of life. Our physical and symbolic separation of the corpse from other living beings is a symbolic marker enabling us to repress or forget the fact that the life that animates our body will necessarily be transmitted to another, will migrate elsewhere, will change its form. This is why one of the founding myths of the religion that has dominated Europe for the last twenty centuries – the myth of the resurrection of the dead – explicitly seeks to affirm, on the one hand, a substantial discontinuity between the life that passes through humanity and that which animates all other living beings and, on the other hand, a personal discontinuity between the life of each individual. The different human bodies in existence divide up life substantially: there are as many lives as there are bodies. On the other hand, human corporeality is *radically different* from that of other living beings – not only because they boast cognitive faculties that others do not have, but because the flesh of human beings does not have the same quality as that of other living beings.

The myth of resurrection in fact developed as a transformation – in Claude Lévi-Strauss's sense of the term, that is, a dialectical modification, a metamorphosis – of the much older myth of reincarnation, which had been in circulation around the Mediterranean for centuries. According to this myth, every life exceeds the limits of the body that harbours it, and is therefore transmitted from body to body. 'Nothing retains its form', as Ovid explains, 'new shapes from old / Nature the great inventor ceaselessly / Contrives', and '[i]n all creation [. . .] / There is no death [. . .] only change / And innovation; what we men call birth / Is but a different new beginning; death / Is but to cease to be the same'.[14] This chain of transformation involves all living beings and the entire planet: 'the sky / And all thereunder changes again and again / We too ourselves, who of this world are part, / Not only flesh and blood but pilgrim souls, / Can make our homes in creatures of the wild / Or of the farm'.[15]

An essential relationship therefore holds between life and corporeality which entails that every individual, after death, must necessarily assume another body, whether human or animal: life, like subjectivity, is not defined by the form through which it passes, so that the subject who says 'I' in human form may be born again – at least in some limited sense – in the body of a rat or a lion. The spirit, the life force, 'roams to and fro, now here, now there, and takes / What frame it will', as Ovid, once again, reminds us, 'passing from beast to man, / From our own form to beast and never dies. / As yielding wax is stamped with new designs / And changes shape and seems not still the same, / Yet is indeed the same, even so our souls / Art still the same for ever, but adopt / In their migrations ever-varying forms'.[16]

Christian resurrection is a distortion of this myth, which is also found in Plato's writings. It promises just one reincarnation rather than an infinite series of them. But this second reincarnation will take place not only *exclusively* in a human body, but in the very body that we have occupied. There is therefore an essential relation not only between subjectivity and its humanity, but above all between subjectivity and individual and personal corporeality. And this is why, from the outset, the debate around the resurrection of the body involves the question of an identity and permanence beyond any nutritional 'accident': the body may be devoured by beasts or worms, but the personal flesh will return. The myth of resurrection is thus the most radical and consequential doctrine of the *human* and *personal* character of our lives, and of the ontological separation between our flesh and that of other living beings.

This then is the purpose served by the sacralization and absolutization of death: it is only because we have made a fetish of our purely human personality and nature – made it an object of absolute faith – that we regard death as an absolute event. The end of our life is never the end of life: every 'corpse' is the transformation, the metamorphosis of life as it changes species, form, mode of existence.

Whenever we claim to be animated by an exclusively and carnally personal, human life that will end with the death of our body, we are not indicating some self-evident fact (after all, in a corpse there is still life, just in other forms); we are professing our faith in the literally *absolute* nature of the human self. To say that there is nothing after death, that the life that animates a body ends with its transformation, is to profess a faith that seeks to contain the subjectivity of the living being within the image that we have made of the human body.

Metamorphosis – in all the forms we have analysed here – is the most powerful objection to any theory which claims there are as many lives as there are bodies, or which affirms a discontinuity between living things in perfect correspondence to the forms of species and individuals. Metamorphosis is a theory of the continuity of life across bodies, a doctrine of the aboriginally multispecies and transcorporeal nature of the self and of life.

Contemporary ecological thinking takes up this position in one of its most astonishing texts. In his most celebrated work, *A Sand County Almanac*, Aldo Leopold, one of the greatest thinkers of the last century, composed a narrative in which he rewrote Homer's *Odyssey* in the form of a diptych depicting the life of two atoms and the journeys that allow them to return to what could be considered their home.[17] In the first episode, the atom in question, given the fictitious name X, lives in an unspoiled landscape untouched by human life. After having 'marked time in the limestone ledge since the Paleozoic seas covered the land', 'locked in a rock' for what seems an endless eternity, X was freed 'when a bur-oak root nosed down a crack and began prying and sucking'. It was then that 'in the flash of a century' X's life 'was pulled out and up into the world of living things';[18] X then went through a series of transformations which saw him incarnated in a flower, an acorn, a deer, an Amerindian, and then back into the soil, only to enter into a rootlet of bluestem grass, etc., until he returned to 'his ancient prison, the sea'.[19] In the second episode, we read of how the atom named Y was released from the mother rock at the moment when 'a new animal had arrived and begun redding up the prairie to fit his own notions of law and order'.[20] In this ravaged landscape, atoms that once roamed 'now lie inert, confused, imprisoned in oily sludge'.[21]

Beyond its condemnation of humanity's deadly interference in the lives of other life forms, this narrative provides a new foundation for environmental thinking and ethics as a whole. Adopting the point of view of the atom is not a crude rhetorical device: it is what makes it possible to understand and to demonstrate the absolute continuity, both material and spiritual (subjective), of all life on this planet. We cannot stop at affirming the reciprocal interdependence of beings, the fact that they make up a system: all beings are the expression of one and the same life, are in a relationship of continuity and not mere spatial contiguity. Discontinuity is not ontological (death), but purely modal and formal: X and Y – Leopold's atoms – change their mode of being, not their substance. As the *logion* at the end of the first atomic portrait says, '[t]he only certain truth' is that the prairie's 'creatures must suck hard, live fast, and die often, lest its losses exceed its gains'.[22]

Death is an event that is far more banal and everyday than might be suggested by the myths we have fabricated for ourselves. We should indeed live fast and die often rather than ending up fetishizing the form that life has temporarily chosen: this form is a mode, not a substance. Such an approach may provide the basis for a radically different attitude towards the planet. For not only does everything around us participate in the life that passes through us with the same intensity, as we are of the same flesh and life as everything that populates this planet, but above all any landscape, no matter how 'natural' or 'artificial', is just an open-air archive of our past and future bodies. We share the same flesh and the same spirit as everything on Earth.

It is easy to imagine the material continuity of the

universe: we have no problem acknowledging that our flesh comes from elsewhere, and that it has inhabited this planet for much longer than our birth. All of our atoms have provided a body for thousands of lives before ours – human, vegetable, bacterial, viral, animal – and will give rise to others, in an unstoppable dance.

However, we are troubled by the idea that this continuity may also apply on a spiritual and speculative level. And yet this transmigration of the self is far more common and everyday than we think. Throughout this book, and at this very moment, I am thinking in you, I am saying 'I' in your mind, just as, when I listen attentively to a friend, my self is occupied by the self of another. Every time we voice, for example, the famous Cartesian saying *cogito ergo sum*, I think therefore I am, for a moment we allow the spirit of Descartes to be reincarnated in us, we lend him our voice, our body, our experience. It is he who says 'I' in us, in a sense thereby contradicting his own argument: the self is not a substance, it does not have a personal structure, it is more like a musical theme that ceaselessly invades minds and colonizes bodies without ever allowing itself to be definitively adopted by any one body rather than another. Every idea is an itinerant self, just like Leopold's atoms. Every self is a carrier of the spirit of others: of their ideas, their life force, their past. It is only thanks to this capacity for psychic transmigration – or, to use the old technical theological term, metempsychosis – that something like a community is possible.

Genetics and Reincarnation

You only have to examine each body to see it: every living being is a huge recycling operation carried out on the lives that preceded it. Nothing that inhabits us is new. Everything comes from other bodies, other places, other times. Living beings are constantly exchanging matter, ideas, and forms, constructing their bodies and minds from those of others. Everything belonged to another life, everything has already lived many times in many forms, everything has been adapted, rearranged, reformed. That is why every life has already transgressed the boundaries between kingdoms, species, and individuals, but also between places and times. Everything that lives, lives by metamorphosis: a transformative repetition of what has gone before. Although it may have behind it an infinity of other lives, nothing that lives within us today has ever lived this particular life before. The recycling that metamorphosis imposes upon the slightest part of this world's matter is what prevents any kind of cycle, any kind of return of the identical. Which is why we should instead speak of reincarnation.

Reincarnation does not imply a straightforward copy of the life that went before. It is a technique that allows two beings to reincarnate themselves in each other's bodies. Apart from eating, sex – even when not associated with reproduction, as in the *Paramecium* – is the most extreme form of transmigration, the one that makes of every living being the shared flesh of other living beings. This feast of transmigration that makes nature an endless carnival means that each living thing is a bastard child, something radically, ontologically impure, hybrid, bearing in its deepest core an element of non-life, the mineral flesh of the planet.

But there is something even more profound that makes our lives an infinite sequence of multiple reincarnations: genes. For the genes that shape our bodies are not just mere information, they are also real microscopic writers, *copywriters* in a very particular sense. Unlike what happens when we write, unlike what happens to me as I write this text, these microscopic writers coincide with their own writings and with the writing process itself. *They write*, but *they are materially* what they write. They are a form of writing that is engendered by the body of the writer and is never separate from it, as if all the words I had written were to travel with me, inscribed within my body. Or rather, the genes are editors for whom the act of writing coincides with a surgical practice on their own bodies: they constantly reinvent and reformulate one another's writing, and the meaning of their writing corresponds to what they manage to do with the body. It is a form of creative writing – literally, as if every word I wrote irreversibly changed my body. Since there is no difference between the speaker and the word spoken, between the subject and the information it imparts, novelty can only emerge through a metamorphosis. Or, conversely, thanks to genes, writing becomes an ontological process of reincarnation. At least two or three things follow from this.

First of all, for genes, to speak, to say 'I', to write, always means to replicate *themselves*. If we have a genetic structure, it is because any information about ourselves or the organism we are part of – that is, any identity – is a replica, a copy, a secondary version. But this chain of reincarnation is as if fragmented and multiplied kaleidoscopically. Thanks to the genes, every detail of our identity is rendered autonomous, separated from all the others, and can be dispersed into an infinite number of lives and bodies. The smallest element of what we are has been capable of living outside us, indifferent to any other element that accompanies it now, and it will be able to reincarnate itself indefinitely in hundreds of other individuals, not necessarily of the same species. The identity produced by reincarnation is always a dissemination that makes of each living being a simultaneous meeting of several peoples, but also a promise of a future life entirely different from the present one.

Fundamentally, genetic writing – the writing of reincarnation – enables us to better understand what it means to speak. We should not approach genetics by way of the metaphor of language, but vice versa: language does to the mind what genes do to bodies. The word divides a mind up into portions that can be reincarnated anywhere, separately from all the other words that accompany or may have accompanied them. Every conversation, every act of thinking, is an exchange of spiritual identity, a mosaic of personalities and little selves that come from elsewhere and are in continual motion.

The Shadow of the Species

Having sold his shadow to the devil, Peter Schlemihl is condemned to permanent exile. After rejecting the devil's second offer, Peter buys a pair of boots which turn out to be seven-league boots. He then withdraws to Tibet to become an anchorite, devoting the rest of his life to the study of nature. 'My *Historia Stirpium Plantarum utriusque Orbis* has appeared', Peter writes to the true author of the famous tale, Adelbert von Chamisso, 'being but a large fragment of my *Flora universalis Terræ*, and a companion to my *Systema Naturæ*. In that I believe I have not only increased the number of known species more than a third (moderately speaking), but have thrown some light on the general system of nature, and the geography of plants.'[23] This fictional character's hopes and dreams as a naturalist were in reality those of the author himself. A medical student, son of the director and co-founder of the Berlin Zoological Museum, Martin Heinrich Carl von Lichtenstein, Chamisso is one of the most extraordinary and ambiguous characters in German Romanticism. Born in Champagne, named Louis Charles Adélaïde de Chamisso de Boncourt, he fled France in 1792 following the Revolution and took refuge in Germany. He once described himself as follows:

> I am a Frenchman in Germany and a German in France, a Catholic among Protestants and a Protestant among Catholics, a philosopher among believers and a pious man among freethinkers, a man of the world among scholars, a pedant among men of the world, a Jacobin among aristocrats and a noble among democrats, a man of the ancien regime, etc. I belong to no one, I am a stranger everywhere, I wanted to embrace everything, everything escapes me.[24]

If *Peter Schlemihl's Miraculous Story* is one of the most profound reflections on those invisible metamorphoses that can play a part in human lives, Chamisso was later to discover one of the most mysterious metamorphic phenomena on Earth. In August 1815, a few months after the publication of his novel, Chamisso embarked at Copenhagen to join the *Rurik*, a ship that had left St Petersburg at the end of July, in the company of the doctor and entomologist Johann Friedrich Eschscholtz and the painter Ludwig Choris. On the way, Chamisso and Eschscholtz became fascinated by salps, pelagic tunicates with gelatinous bodies, and made an important discovery. In the words of Chamisso himself, they discovered that

> in these transparent molluscs of the high seas, one and the same species is represented in alternate generations in two very different forms, namely an individual salp that swims freely gives birth to young beings which have a different structure, almost like a polyp, chained to each other, and each in this republic of aggregated individuals then gives birth to individual free-swimming animals, in which the form of the previous generation returns.[25]

This is a most amazing discovery because, as Chamisso says, 'it is as if the caterpillar were to give birth to the butterfly and the butterfly in turn gave birth to the caterpillar'.[26] On his return from the trip, he published the book *De animalibus quibusdam e classe vermium Linnaeana in circumnavigatione Terrae: De Salpa* [*On Certain Animals Belonging to the Linnaean Class of Vermium: The Salp*], in which he describes the discovery in more detail. Salps, he writes, 'exist in a twofold form, because the descendants are different from their parents throughout their lives, but capable of producing a new generation that is the same as them'. For this reason, 'each salp is different from the mother and from the daughter, but is identical to its grandmothers and grandchildren and to its sisters'. The two generations also differ in that the first is solitary, while the second involves an aggregation of individuals. One might think that the solitary progeny is the animal and the aggregated progeny is more like a chain of living eggs. But on closer examination, Chamisso continues, it seems more comparable to the metamorphosis of insects or frogs:

> If it weren't so common, we might be surprised by this metamorphosis of unchanging forms, independent of the life course of each individual, which gives rise to two different forms which develop later, the larva and the imago. This metamorphosis of form occurs in a metamorphosis into two successive generations, with the form changing not in the individual or in the offspring but across the generations.[27]

The reason why the generations differ as the larva differs from the imago remains rather obscure. Chamisso's discovery was at first heavily criticized (in particular by Lorenz Oken), but unexpected confirmation of it came from biologist Michael Sars, who identified other marine animals that appear to display the same form of 'intergenerational metamorphosis'. The most important case is that of the common jellyfish (known today by the scientific name *Aurelia aurita*). Sars writes that, in all such cases, 'it is not the individual but the generation that is undergoing metamorphosis'.[28] But it was a Danish biologist, Johannes Japetus Smith Steenstrup, who would coin the phrase which, from the time of his publication, came to define the phenomenon in question: 'alternation of generations'. Steenstrup defines it as a

> remarkable and thus far inexplicable natural phenomenon of an animal producing an offspring which at no time resembles its mother, but which, on the other hand, itself produces offspring that return in form and nature to the mother, so that the mother animal does not find her likeness in her own brood but in her second, third or fourth generation offspring.[29]

Steenstrup sees the role of one generation as being to 'prepare the way for the next generation of animals destined to reach a higher degree of perfection': this is what he calls the nursemaid (*Ammen*) generation. It was Steenstrup who removed this phenomenon from the register of anomalies: citing Goethe's assertion that 'nature follows its own path, and what seems to us to be an exception is the rule', he strives to demonstrate that 'we must no longer consider [alternation of generations] as something paradoxical or deviant, as we have hitherto been too inclined to interpret it, and the phenomena in which it manifests itself'.[30]

Unlike many naturalists such as Leuckart in 1853, who interpreted alternation of generations as 'a metamorphosis spread over several generations', Steenstrup differentiates between metamorphosis and alternation of generations. And, following the English biologist Owen, we call 'the cycle of change, which being carried through a succession of individuals and not completed in a single life-time [. . .] a "metagenesis" rather than a "metamorphosis"'.[31] Today this is still the term used to refer to the phenomenon of alternation between a sexual haploid stage and an asexual diploid stage in plants, while for animals the term 'heterogamy' is more often used to designate an alternation between parthenogenetic generation and sexual generation.

Yet it is Steenstrup who furnishes the most profound reflection on this phenomenon. If there are alternating generations, he says, it is because 'the species is not fully represented by adult individuals of both sexes capable of reproduction, nor by their development: so it is necessary to have individuals from one or more previous generations, which are like a complement to them'.[32] If normally, in nature, the species is represented by the individual and by the metamorphosis that takes place in its development, in this case we could see a kind of 'lack of complete individuality as representatives of species', a deficit of 'species individuality'.[33]

A species needs metamorphosis because no individual form can ever exhaust it. The life of any species is basically a very long history of successive and parallel reincarnations: it needs to reincarnate every form in others. On the other hand, none of the forms that a species goes through expresses that species – or we could say that it expresses it too much: we are always less or more than human. The same applies to species in relation to the life that passes through them: none of them can contain the substance of life entirely, none can exhaust its force and individuality. Like Peter Schlemihl, life on the planet has sold its shadow to the devil, and is now obliged to travel from place to place and from form to form.

4
MIGRATIONS

Planetary Migration

The real subject of all metamorphosis is our planet. All living things are nothing more than a recycling of its body, a patchwork built from ancestral material. It is through us and in each one of us that the Earth can say 'I'. The life of the planet is an immense and unstoppable metamorphosis. And the primary way in which we perceive its metamorphic force is through the migration it imposes upon each of its inhabitants.

Imagine that we are in a bus, a car, a plane, a ship, or a train. But this vehicle is so large that we have no idea what its shape is or where its boundaries lie.

We've been there for so long that we've forgotten how and when we got on board (as if we had been there for ever) and even why we took this means of transport. We don't know or have forgotten its destination, even once we arrive.

Like a cruise ship, this vessel is so populous that we don't even know who the pilot is, or if there is anyone at the helm at all.

If we imagine all this, we will have quite an accurate picture of what it means to be in the world. The first characteristic of the world is not in fact that of being an immense mass of extended matter, nor that of being an open and receptive space, just as it is not defined by being populated by a multiplicity of 'other' objects and subjects. Nor does its essence reside in being or becoming an object of knowledge, in opposing itself to the subject as that which opens itself to the senses and to thought.

No, the world is defined first and foremost by the fact that it is a *planet*, i.e. a body, or rather a set of bodies characterized by irregular and almost perpetual motion: the word 'planet' comes from the Greek root *planaomai*, which means 'to wander, to become lost'. The world is the very being of metamorphosis: not just the theatre of a transformation that concerns a limited and marginal portion of its body, but the *cause, form, and matter of metamorphosis itself and of its movement.* It is because of this *planetary* nature that nothing can remain where it is, nor what it is. Look at everything around you, regardless of its texture, shape, age, or consistency. The birds, the wind, the rivers, but also the buildings, the smells, the colours: everything moves, everything changes. Everything changes places, even if we do not perceive it. Everything changes form even if this transformation remains invisible to our eyes. The world as a planetary reality is a *wandering* body and, inversely, wandering is the primary attribute of all bodies in this universe, terrestrial and celestial alike. Wandering is not just a spatial movement: it does not just refer to movement from one place to another. It is a far more intimate, corporeal movement that is at work at all levels of the life of every earthly being. Sex and nutrition, but also imagination, language, birth, and death are all forms and expressions of this movement. It is because of the *planetary* nature of Gaia and all of her children that every body on Earth is subject to metamorphosis.

But it is only by way of this planetary nature – this metamorphic force that defines the being of even the smallest particle of the globe – that this disparate set of objects, beings, modes, or events adds up to something unitary: everything sooner or later occupies the place of the other (and cannot do otherwise), every being must sooner or later enter the body of the other (or become it). The form of others will necessarily become our form. Everything participates in the same body, the same substance, the same nature. Thanks to the metamorphosis that runs through it, each being is rendered planetary, and therefore worldly: wandering is the cosmic name for metamorphosis in its most original, elementary, mineral form.

Any cosmology, any doctrine of the world – any theory of metamorphosis – must embrace this planetary dimension. Every cosmology must be a planetology, a metaphysics of wandering. Every being, as a child of Gaia, is a drifter – changing, moving home, migrating. The world obliges all of its parts to be constantly on the move, it forces everything, living and non-living, stone, water, air, fire, elephants, men, oaks, and viruses, to move, to change, to metamorphose on the spot and to transform, by metamorphosis, that which surrounds them.

This wandering motion can show itself anywhere, at any time, and involves several dimensions; it occurs at several levels, simultaneously, to the point where everything, literally everything, wanders along different and contradictory trajectories.

The first dimension – the simplest, most common, and most obvious, yet which is the object of constant repression – is the geological: before any other transformation, before any other migration, before any other displacement of the living, there is a more originary, more universal migration, the one that involves and implicates the Earth beneath our feet. That space we continue to call, as a sign of our cultural and psychological repression, *terra firma*.

In 1912 a German climatologist discovered that nothing is fixed and stable on Earth: there is no firm ground because every piece of land is being dragged elsewhere, and is gradually moving from its current position. The lithosphere has a dynamic that seems not so far removed from what we might imagine to be that of the circulation of meteors in the atmosphere: Earth and sky are subject to a common self-transformation. Alfred Wegener, the first theorist of 'continental drift', profoundly revolutionized geology: today his intuitions are considered the equivalent in geology of what Darwin's theory represents in biology.

Plate tectonics is the destruction of geography as a formal science. There is no longer an Earth, there are no longer any stable and definitive forms. All continents are movable rafts, ships carrying living things from one side of the planet to the other, above and below its surface. From a planetary point of view, life migrates, since the very Earth upon which every living thing stands is moving. It is impossible to think of migrants as a subset of the living. The ground is what migrates, and never stops migrating. There is no homeland or colony, only different boats or rafts. Every continent, every land (as well as every ocean), is a kind of Noah's Ark carrying a myriad of living beings elsewhere, far from any origin. The difference being that this journey will never come to an end, because the movement is not the result of a flood or an accidental climatic event. The very condition of being in the world is that of migration: not a journey from one place to another but a kind of perpetual motion – a wandering or drifting. Plate tectonics, the idea that everything on Earth is drifting, universalizes the very idea contained in the concept of planet, that of a body in continuous irregular motion. Every body on Earth has the same status and participates in the same dynamic as the Earth as a whole. Accepting the planetary nature of every living being therefore means radicalizing the fact that it shares its deepest nature with Gaia.

Metamorphosis, so intimate a part of the living being, is a consequence of this drift that animates and continually reshapes the body of the Earth. Conversely, the metamorphosis of living beings, rather than disturbing the life of the planet, constitutes its essential dynamic: it is by metamorphosing that matter can become a planet, perpetually wandering and drifting.

Our drift is multifaceted. First of all, from an astronomical point of view, the Earth is the metamorphosis of the same nebula of matter from which the Sun and the other planets were formed. But also, from a microscopic point of view, the drift is not just geological and geographical, it is also biological and physiological. Or, more precisely, sex and evolution, but also food and metabolism, are just an extension of the movement of the metamorphic life of the planet. We are wandering, drifting beings, and we can be drifting beings because, and only because, together we make up a supercontinent, a living superbeing whose parts are constantly drifting apart and colliding with one another.

Vehicle Theory

The *planetary* condition is not a quality of the individual: to be a planet always means to be a planet for something or someone else. Every object in the world is something else's planet. Every living being is the planet of some other living being. The Earth is our planet: it carries us, constantly transports us elsewhere. But we are a planet for many other beings: for the bacteria, fungi, and viruses that live in our bodies, for instance. We are also planetary from a genetic point of view: the human body is an aggregate of pieces of genetic code from other times, other species, other forms of life. I myself am the planet of the genetic codes of my mother and father, codes which, through my body, have wandered far beyond the anatomical space of their bodies. Genetics, then, is a planetary tectonics of life. Equally, ideas and knowledge are our planets (since they support us), but also the inhabitants of human planets (because we spread them everywhere).

More generally, any relationship to other beings reproduces this planetary configuration, where one being becomes the planet for another, where they are one another's planet in various ways. The metamorphic relationship is always a planetary relationship, in the twofold sense that it transforms an object into a world and makes the forms in question one another's planets. This relational dimension of planetary being is what we call a vehicle. The fact that everything is the planet for something else means that everything is the vehicle for something else: the universe, the whole world, is a metaphor, a transportation device, in which everything moves and bears something else upon it. Everything is a Noah's Ark. To be in the world is to bear something other than oneself and to be borne, transported, by others. So that the metaphysics of wandering is also a metaphysics of vehicularity. The difference between the two terms is that whereas in one we are talking about the inner movement of a body, in the other each planet is not only a moving body, but a body that imparts movement to other bodies.

In this sense, a car, a boat, or a plane are the most elementary and paradigmatic forms of being-in-the-world: living beings, but also all objects, are vehicles that carry what they bear to some other place. This intuition was the basis of a very ancient doctrine, the Platonic concept of the *ochema*, the vehicle, which is the condition of possibility for all forms of terrestrial and ultra-terrestrial existence of the soul. In several of his works Plato referred to a vehicle that accompanies and makes possible the descent of the soul into the body and all forms of incarnation. He speaks of it in the *Timaeus*, where he imagines that the great craftsman responsible for the creation of the world assigned a star to each human soul, and, having 'mounted each soul in a carriage, as it were [. . .] showed it the nature of the universe'.[1] Elsewhere, he speaks of how, after death, souls are transported to the Acheron in their vehicle. The Platonic school speculated a great deal about these details, and imagined various 'soul carriages'. Thought of as a vehicle, the body does not define a geographical or physical adhesion to a place, a space, or a piece of matter; on the contrary, it is what makes movement possible – it is the condition of possibility of exiting space and place, or, better, the principle of their permanent variation. We have a body not so as to better stick to a here and now, but so as to be able to change place, time, and space, to change form, to change matter. The body-vehicle is the condition of possibility of metamorphosis: it is what makes it possible to go elsewhere, to become other.

Our body is just a car, an aeroplane, a ship for identities and forms. A car that has made it possible for the identities of an infinite number of other individuals to come out of their shells and live in us. An aeroplane for an infinity of memories and ideas that can go anywhere, traversing place and matter. A ship of images of the world that are in the process of changing the nature of the world. Every body is a journey in progress. And as in the Platonic tradition, even after death, souls never stop travelling, they just change their vehicle, their carriage.

This amounts to an inversion of the logic of substance and locality: there is no substrate, and being borne by the other means undertaking a journey. To enter into another life is to be taken elsewhere. To become something, everything must become the planet of something else: everything must accept entering into a vehicular relation with others. On the one hand, the relationship to the world is always mediated by another body: there is no simple, immediate existence, and there is never an immediate relationship to reality. On the other hand, being part of a body does not simply mean being mixed with one body, but being drawn by it into an infinity of other bodies and other places. Every body is a corridor. Every body is the gateway to an infinity of other worlds.

The Great Ark

> [E]very beast, according to its kind, and all the livestock according to their kinds, and every creeping thing that creeps on the earth, according to its kind, and every bird, according to its kind, every winged creature. They went into the ark with Noah, two and two.

The Old Testament gives us to think of the whole globe as one huge vehicle. However, any vehicular logic makes it impossible to think totality in spatial terms: if there are vehicles, it is because there is no common space, no common house, no place of cohabitation that would allow a stable relationship for all, especially in one and the same place. If we must continue to wander and drift, it is because the place that would allow all objects to meet can never exist. The world is a planet, and for that reason it is neither a globe nor a house. The world is a planet, and that is why there will always be an elsewhere and an otherwise. To understand this, all it takes is a thought experiment.

Imagine seeing all the species on Earth gathered together in one place, of their own free will rather than by divine command. Imagine them moving *all together*, *one beside the other* towards this space. Imagine them coming from the most remote places – walking, flying, crawling. Imagine insects and birds, viruses and bacteria, imagine all trees and plants extending their bodies and sending out their seeds. Imagine this Assembly of the Living, the Commune of Life. Life as an actual, sensible encounter of all living beings.

Imagine this place. What space could possibly house all these living creatures? How can we think this kind of paradise, no longer open only to humans but to all species? How can we think the place in which all of the living could be brought together? Where would its borders lie? To think this absolute landscape, we would have to imagine all beings not just constrained to be in a relationship of reciprocal contiguity: in order for them all to be in the same place, they would have to be one on top of the other, one with the other, one within the other.

This absolute landscape, the landscape that unites all living things, would then be the landscape or frontier that separates one species from another, one body from another: a threshold. In this landscape, every skin, every cuticle, would be what allows each species to transform itself into the other, a corridor through which every body becomes the body of the other. In this place every living being could also live the life of the other.

This absolute landscape is not, and could never be, a specific place on Earth: there would always be others living elsewhere. There would be other pieces of Gaia that would remain unrepresented. Nor can it coincide with the totality of the Earth: the planet is too vast for all of us to see one another, to live on one another's breath. And this is why the living have invented another way of convening the Assembly: instead of reserving a single space for the convention of the living, they have distributed this assembly – distributing the absolute landscape throughout all the bodies of the living. Each living being constitutes an intensity of this new Noah's Ark that allows us to meet the other within our own bodies. Each one of us is the physical meeting-place of several species, each one of us is a little zoo that always carries many more species than the one to which we imagine we belong. Life has made each living being an ark for an infinite number of living and non-living beings. Everything becomes a landscape.

It is to make the existence of this ark possible, and to make it coincide with the bodies of all living beings – the smallest as well as the largest – that life has taken on the form in which we know it. Birth and death, for example, are there to allow each person to be an ark: being born always means becoming part of the life of another body, having it as your vehicle for nine months, and then becoming the vehicle, the ark of its genetic identity, its life force, its memory, for the rest of your life.

Evolution is also a way of structuring all species like a Noah's Ark: a species is introduced, i.e. borne into the world, by another species of which it will ultimately become the ark. Thus, we humans were introduced to Gaia by way of the ark of the great apes: the primates were our ark, and we are now theirs.

Life is not a quality peculiar to certain bodies, it is just the consequence of the vehicular nature of matter, of the planetary structure of this world. There is life only where bodies are vehicles, arks, planets for one another. In this world – our world – space can never be pure extension; it never presents itself as something given. There is no space, there is only travel. There is only life.

We must learn to see every living being as an ancestral ark. These arks traverse the history of the planet and the cosmos, not just their geographies: they traverse the totality of apparent boundaries – those that seem to separate the living from the non-living, those that we suspect to exist between matter and spirit or between individuals, species, places, and times.

They do not pre-exist the world. On the contrary, they produce it, they fabricate it, they embody it. It's impossible to know whether it is a question of a single ark that has expanded so far that we can no longer locate its origin, or a multiplicity of arks that have become so entangled in each other that they have merged into one.

Through these crossings, they bring into coexistence the most distant places on Earth, but also distant and incompatible times, or forms of life that have no common kinship. It is because of them that every being on Earth carries in its body elements that are prehistoric and others that are hypermodern. The newborn, the newest living being to emerge into the world – whether human or cetacean, dragonfly or oak tree – is made of material that inhabited this planet before the appearance of any life form. Its body is older than its species or family, and yet it may forever alter the history of the cosmos at a much later point in its true existence. None of what endows it with life comes, strictly speaking, from the place where it was born: its ultra-millennia-old atoms have travelled all over the universe, have come from places that no longer exist and will end up in places that probably have not yet emerged. There is nothing autochthonous in the living, there is nothing absolutely autochthonous in the matter of our world.

And these arks continue to scramble the archives and cartographies that would allow us to describe a clear-cut history and geography of the cosmos. They are always either ahead or behind, they never stay put. They make it impossible to synchronize times or to lock down and seal places. They make it impossible to assume that past history is more important than the future to defining the identity of any being. They make it impossible to distinguish our own childhood from that of the world.

We carry within us the childhood of the universe – or, better, we share our childhood with every least particle of matter on this planet and everything around it. We share our breath with all living things present and future. It is Gaia who breathes in us. Each breath of a new being produces more sharing and a more common body: we once again remix the body of the whole planet and build new alliances between forms. Each living being is a micro-Leviathan, each one a different assembly of the most disparate and heterogeneous bodies.

This ancientness, this vitality, is not just an attribute. It is the mark and the substance of the fragility of every form: everything that exists carries within itself the need to change its skin, its face, and is animated by a life that can never be contained within its limits. What we mistakenly think of as vulnerability, mortality, or weakness, is only the flipside of this openness and continuity between all lives: each of us has a life that is not perfectly suited to the body we inhabit. It is just waiting for the moment when it can be transformed into another body. This ancient, omnivorous hybrid life force is already migrating elsewhere. And more generally, mortality is only the proof that, at the heart of every life, there is a mineral matter – the matter of Gaia – which has no particular need to animate this or that body: mineral matter, indifferent to forms and yet available to all. These mineral entrails that all life has softened in its bosom clamour to become rock again. Metamorphosis does not mean immortality – not even for the planet.

Everybody in the House

It is in terms of this vehicularity that we should describe and understand our being together. But we are afraid of vehicles. We are frightened of arks. We fear the journey. In spite of everything, we find it difficult to free ourselves of our obsession with home. We cannot escape our love for neat, clean, orderly spaces that are ours, ours alone and not for others. We cannot free ourselves from our love for clear boundaries, for the opposition between an inner and an outer space: we continue to prefer the inside, the cave, the bowels of the Earth, to exposure to the sun, wind, and rain – to the world. The house is the archetype of the boundary, not only because it includes the first walls that we build, use, and live within, but because it is through the house that we separate out humanity into the close, intimate, and inseparable, and the rest. It is thanks to the house that there is a me and a you and a difference between them; it is through the house that the self learns to no longer separate itself from certain 'others' but to amalgamate with them, to become familiar with them. We find it hard to leave the house, to take leave of the idea that it represents a *natural* relationship to space, immediate and original rather than artificial and accidental. We can never manage to free ourselves of the idea that there is somewhere we are safe from harm, where we are naturally protected, where we are *naturally* ourselves.

This obsession with home is much more profound than it seems. Not only does it structure our political experience (each of us claims the right to have a home), since the city is only a collection of houses; not only does it structure our experience of things (the so-called 'economy' is nothing but the attempt to identify the individual with the household). It also, above all, defines the way in which we continue to think about the relationship between living beings, and between living beings and the space that surrounds them. Indeed, it is on this idea that all of ecology is based, or at least was originally constituted. For not all reflections on the living, it seems, have managed to free themselves from a childish nostalgia for the idea of nature as an immense, natural, welcoming, benevolent *home*, a *family* where there are only sisters, brothers, fathers, friends, and never any real strangers. Ecology as a whole testifies to a will to make the ark impossible, and to instead recognize and reproduce everywhere the form of the house – the opposite of the vehicle. The very term 'ecology' already confesses this predilection for the domestic.

The term first appeared in an 1866 monograph by Ernst Haeckel on the general morphology of organisms, as a variation of an older term (at least a century older), 'natural economics'. 'Ecology', writes Haeckel, 'is the science of natural economics', or 'a branch of physiology that does not even appear in textbooks':[2] namely, the 'physiology of the reciprocal relations of organisms between themselves and with their environment'.[3] However, ecological science can only set itself up independently of other scientific disciplines or other points of view on reality – physical biology, chemistry, or geology, for example – to the extent that it imagines these relations as irreducible to mere facts, whether biological (the mere extension of individual metabolism), physical (pure thermodynamic mechanism), or chemical (simple molecular equilibrium). For these relations to be the subject of a new, different, and autonomous science, they must be of a different nature. This relationship, which is not purely biological, chemical, geological, or physical, between the various living species and between these species and each of their own worlds, is of a social nature: ecology began as a theory of non-human societies, or of the social connection of non-human beings to the abiotic natural world. As Frederic Clements and Victor Shelford put it in 1930: 'Ecology is in large measure the science of community populations.'[4] From the beginning, its question has been the particularity of non-human sociability, but this sociability has always been modelled on the human home. This is already evident in the work of Haeckel, according to whom the condition of possibility of ecology is 'the limitation of the conditions of existence of organisms, whatever their species'.[5] This limitation is twofold: firstly geographical, because 'no one can live anywhere on Earth'[6] – all living creatures are confined to one part of the globe, and most of them to a particularly restricted space. This limitation in turn stems from the reciprocal relationships between organisms, because 'every species of organism is dependent on many others that live in the same place and that are harmful, indifferent or useful to it'.[7] Scarcity, however, is less a quantitatively proven fact than a condition of possibility: each animal or living being's access to resources is socially mediated by other non-human individuals. That is to say, ecology has to reflect on the scarcity of conditions of existence in order to be able to think about the social (and not purely chemical or thermodynamic) nature of the relationship to the environment: only when resources are scarce can one speak of competition. In fact, it is this set of limits that justifies the idea that this set of reciprocal relations must be considered as a household (*Haushalt*): nature is an economy in the old sense of the word, a system within which everything and everyone must have a meaning and a function. Everything in this economy is defined according to its utility. The biological world is structured like the most basic social order that obtains between humans: the household. And if totemism, according to Lévi-Strauss's famous definition, 'postulates a logical equivalence between a society of natural species and a world of social groups' in such a way that '[n]atural and social groupings are homologous [. . .] and the selection of a grouping in one order involves the adoption of the corresponding grouping in the other',[8] then ecology is already, in its very name, a kind of anti-totemism that tries to prove that everything in non-humans is structured like the basic domestic social unit of humans. We have long had a common tendency to project our own experience of the social onto plants and animals. It could be said that ecology was born as an incomplete science of non-human sociality: incomplete because it has never succeeded in thinking beyond the domestic paradigm. Without being fully aware of it, in its general structure, in its orientation, in its fundamental concepts, ecology has constituted a strange invitation to imagine non-human living beings within the boundaries of the home. All are at home and must remain there until their death. If one of them leaves their home (their eco-system), that can only mean an invasion of a foreign territory or the disruption of an equilibrium. In its attempt to question the relationship between living beings, ecology ended up projecting out of the cities – into the spaces of the so-called 'wild' – a very bourgeois, very nineteenth-century order of life. You stay at home, you don't go out, and space is defined by the laws of property and cleanliness. In trying to safeguard the non-human, ecology has ended up as one of the world's greatest agencies for the anthropomorphizing and humanization of the non-human. Thanks to ecology, the world is like an immense allotment garden where all life forms politely respect the boundaries.

The Domestic Life of Non-Humans

It was not modern ecology, however, that first imposed upon living beings the metaphor of a strictly domestic indoors relationship to life forms and the territory they occupy. Another discipline, of which ecology is a sort of unconscious reincarnation, preceded it: the economy of nature. The first historical evidence of this science is the 1749 doctoral thesis of Isaak Biberg, a student of Carl von Linnaeus. According to Biberg, the economy of nature is 'the most wise disposition of natural beings instituted by the sovereign creator according to which they tend towards common ends and have reciprocal functions'.[9] Here, 'disposition', as Linnaeus acknowledges in other texts, is the technical term used in theology to refer to divine providence. This doctrine therefore stipulates that every being has its own place in the great household of the world, a place granted to it by the head of the family, God.

From this point of view, the economy of nature is therefore a branch of Christian theology, it is the discipline that investigates the relationship between God and living beings. Or rather, the relationship that all living beings entertain with one another and with the material world on the basis of a sovereign decision made by their Creator. And this is no coincidence: in a world where species are supposed to be fixed and to have no genealogical relationship with one another, it is impossible to think that an American horse and a European dog, which will never meet, could have any reciprocal relationship unless one places oneself in the position of their common Creator, who created both and who is therefore capable of understanding their mutual relationship.

It is only from the Creator's point of view that the natural world appears and can appear as a *society*, an order of actors following a logic that is not purely material. And so, since it is only from the Creator's point of view that the question of the mutual relationship between living beings – of the society of non-humans – can even be asked, the model for thinking about this society must be that of the home. Indeed, 'economy' must be understood here in its ancient sense, that is, as the science of the home, of the *oikos*, of the domestic, as opposed to the science of politics. In ancient times, economics was seen as the opposite of politics: one seemed opposed to the other just as the domestic sphere of the *oikos* was opposed to the political sphere of the city and state. The opposition was firstly chronological, and then hierarchical: the household precedes the state because it concerns association as it relates to biological survival, rather than as it relates to spiritual life – it is a more natural community than the *polis*. A household is not opposed to the city as a space without government, but as a different form of government. As Aristotle said, 'Politics is the business of many rulers, the economy of one.'[10] Moreover, whereas politics was based on autonomy and aimed at the freedom of citizens, in antiquity every household presupposed slavery, and did not provide for any real freedom of the subjects in relation to the father's power. Within the household, in fact, things and people were placed on the same level (Aristotle's definition of the slave as a 'living instrument' bears witness to this). Unlike what is the case in the city, where the ruler has power only over humans, in the household the father also and above all has power over things. If freedom is the pivot of politics, on the contrary, the structure of the domestic is defined by utility and order. Everyone has their place, everything has a purpose, everything has its function.

Accordingly, to think of nature in economic terms is to imagine that each living being has its place, its function, its defined role, and that there is an unquestioned transcendental unity that allows us to consider all natural beings as existing in secret harmony. In the words of one of its oldest theorists, Xenophon:

> We agreed that economy was the proper title of a branch of knowledge, and this branch of knowledge appeared to be that whereby men are enabled to enhance the value of their houses or estates; and by this word 'house or estate' we understood the whole of a man's possessions; and 'possessions' again we defined to include those things which the possessor should find advantageous for the purposes of his life; and things advantageous finally were discovered to mean all that a man knows how to use and turn to good account.[11]

In a Christian context, God is the creator of the world, not just the king or governor: he can exercise power over the world and all its living beings only because he is the father of them all. The relationship between God and the world is the same as that between the head of a family and his household; God's power over the world is the power of government of the head of a family: an economic power. Everything in the world must be considered part of the household, because only within this order does everything acquire a function. The natural world is organized like a huge household, a domestic space, rather than as a site of politics: there is no autonomy or negotiation of the site that everyone is supposed to occupy, because everyone has already been assigned a task and a function. Thus, whenever we think that the association of non-humans is constituted according to the logic of utility and order (whenever we think of nature as a big house, a space where there is no negotiation or contingency), this is not an observation but a repetition of the old anti-totemic gesture that gave birth to ecological knowledge.

It is also because of this social, purely domestic paradigm that ecology thinks the sphere of the non-human in purely patrimonial terms. 'Everything which a man possesses [. . .] forms part of his household',[12] as Xenophon wrote, and God's 'economic' government of the world makes non-humans into a set of goods defined entirely by their utility.

It is therefore no coincidence that the primary consequence of this origin is that ecology and the market economy share a common epistemological framework and language. Another student of Linnaeus makes an explicit comparison between the economics of goods and that of non-humans:

> A truly wonderful economy has been established on our globe [. . .] so that they all follow one another in turn as if in a chain. For just as in our private economy neither the plough, nor the fence, nor the dung heap are suitable as food or medicine, but are nonetheless of very great use, so also in the economy of nature many things have been prepared which are of very great use in a mediate way, though not immediately. Men count their economy among

> the greatest inventions they could imagine: but I bid you consider how admirable is the economy established by the wisest of beings himself.[13]

And in the same treatise that founded the economy of nature, Isaak Biberg speaks of invisible hands that allow the natural order to be established: 'In order that natural things may subsist in an uninterrupted series, the wisdom of the sovereign spirit has ordered [. . .] that all natural beings in turn hold out a helping hand for the conservation of any species.'[14] From an epistemological point of view, at least, ecology and capitalism are siblings: they belong to the same family and have interests in common.

The search for an internal order defined by harmony and by a kind of mutual utility is in part a response to the one fact that the early texts of ecology seem to repeat with endless horror: that war is an elementary form of non-human sociality. Daniel Wilcke, another student of Linnaeus, writes that

> if a man [. . .] were to gaze with all his attentive senses upon the terraced globe as upon a new home, he would see the sky covered by countless plants of great diversity intermingled in the greatest confusion and mistreated by worms, insects, fish, amphibians, birds, and mammals, to the point of arousing great compassion: he would see these living beings not only devour the most beautiful flowers, but even, with astonishing tyranny, kill one another pitilessly. In short, he would find nothing there but the war of all against all and, on the other hand, would find himself powerless and exposed to the violence of the greatest number; worried and uncertain, he would find it difficult if not impossible to find anywhere to take refuge. But after a long enough stay in this world, I say, he would gradually distinguish an elementary order, and finally the supreme

> confusion would appear to him as an order so remarkable that, in his astonishment, he would recognize that it is difficult and even futile to seek in the divine work a beginning and an end; for all things exist in circular motion.[15]

The reciprocal relationship between non-humans seems to be a *summum* of violence: a war of all against all (the image, of course, comes from Hobbes) that constantly threatens the physical equilibrium of every species. Thinking of nature as a home serves precisely to deny – or better, to repress – this violence, to integrate it back into a broader, more secret underlying rationality of peace and harmony, a combination of local injuries and universal utility. It is only thanks to these 'invisible hands', to this economy, that, faced with war, there is no need for a pact, a contract, as there is between humans. Among non-humans, each being has a role in a domestic order that it must respect according to its ontological status. This is why thinking of the planet as a home – that is, literally, thinking *ecologically* – makes any kind of terrestrial politics impossible. To imagine an ecological governance of the world means thinking that the reciprocal relationship between non-humans is never the result of a voluntary and contingent negotiation or decision.

This context allows us to fully understand Darwin's theory of evolution. Its most important breakthrough was not just its assertion of the transformation of species (already widely upheld in the eighteenth century, and subsequently taken up by Lamarck), but the belief that the transformation of species is an ecological, i.e. social, phenomenon. The genetic and morphological destiny of each species is not the consequence of purely chemical or geological equilibria, but of phenomena relating to a very specific form of sociality: competition and war.

Rather than removing war from nature by integrating it back into a hidden logic of global utility, Darwin made the war of all against all the proof of a social labour shared by all non-humans, and which allows nature to produce local and global utility. War is the social bond that allows non-human society to improve and expand. It is in this generalized war that genealogy becomes a domestic instrument, a machine for producing utility both locally and globally: it is through artificial selection (humanity's war against nature) that this utility can be exploited, but it is especially through natural selection that the mutual generation of living things produces marginal utility, makes possible the improvement of some species, and enhances the utility of others. Darwinian theory marks both the dissolution and the triumph of the economy of nature and its theological presuppositions: everything, even and above all war and competition between individuals and species, has a function and contributes to the creation of an internal order. War is only a ruse to make the great House yet more powerful and robust than ever.

But metamorphosis operates against all houses.

Invasions

Planet Earth is nothing but the life of metamorphosis, the drift of all living things: its nature is such that everything must change places and every place must change its contents. Ecology is impossible, because nothing can ever remain in place: beings never have a home, and no place will ever be a home for a single owner.

It was one of the fathers of botanical geography who observed that no association of living beings with a place can ever be thought of in terms of autochthony. When he published his monumental *Étude sur la géographie botanique de l'Europe* (*Study of the Botanical Geography of Europe*) in 1854, Henri Lecoq claimed that 'dealing with the sociality of plants and their associations between similar individuals and between different species' would coincide with the study 'of phenomena of migration and colonization'.[16]

Indeed, Lecoq continues, 'rarely does the plant population of a country belong entirely to that country. It comes either from plants actually native to the soil in which they live, or from colonizing species, transported by various means.' In a kind of inverted totemism which has been characteristic of botanical science since its origins, studying 'the area of extension of each species' for Lecoq means 'discovering its true homeland, its travels, its battles, its colonizations', while at the same time 'following step by step the invasion of our plains and mountains by these foreign populations':

> I have endeavoured to follow in their footsteps just as historians seek to discover our origins in the wild hordes which, in remote times, flung themselves upon our old Europe, mixing their vigorous races with the defeated and submissive inhabitants whose heritage they had come to seize.[17]

To socialize, one must migrate, change places, and transform a place. It is impossible to live – that is, to encounter living beings – without travelling. Even those beings that have been considered the paradigm of stability are migrants, as Gilles Clément and Stefano Mancuso would later repeat.

All living beings make their relationship to space a means of metamorphosing themselves and the world they inhabit. Settling in a place means transforming it: a house is only a scar left by some metamorphosis of the world that we have forgotten. Any relationship of prolonged and frequent use of a place and the beings that live there entails a profound change in its nature. Every dwelling is a twofold invasion: we invade the space we inhabit and that space invades us.

Thinking the relationship of living beings to space in terms of autochthony does not therefore mean attaining an origin: rather, it means imposing upon beings a normativity that is extraneous to their actual lives. In fact, the categories that allow us to do this do not come from biological observation but from British common law. It was a nineteenth-century British biologist, Hewett Cottrell Watson, who created this misunderstanding. In investigating British flora, Watson complained of plants 'which have yet acquired a very uncertain right to be incorporated with the proper spontaneous flora of the island', i.e. 'species springing up occasionally from seeds or roots thrown out of gardens, and maintaining themselves a few years; and [. . .] those designedly planted for ornamental or economical purposes. Such are no more entitled to be called Britons, than are the Frenchmen or Germans who occasionally make their homes in England.'[18] A few years later, Watson published a book in which he established 'the civil claims and local situation of [British plant] species in accordance with a scale of terms'.[19] And in an astonishing anti-totemic gesture, he applied the categories of *common law* to plants, distinguishing between native, denizen, and alien species. Whenever ecology persists in talking about 'invasive' species – which it has continued to do, especially following Charles Elton's 1958 work *The Ecology of Invasions by Animals and Plants* – it obliges us to impose upon the plant world the mores and conventions of a geographically and historically minute part of human culture (namely, nineteenth-century British legal culture).

Here a human-all-too-human norm attempts, in various ways, to force onto non-humans social forms typical of nineteenth-century states with closed borders. It is as if ecology requires all non-human species to behave like good family fathers (mindful of order and utility) or like citizens careful not to cross the totally arbitrary national borders that humans have drawn for themselves.

Recognizing the metamorphosis of the Earth means freeing living beings from this strange captivity: they do not just inhabit Gaia, they carry her in their bellies – they take her with them wherever they go. They do not inhabit this or that territory, they are a soil that is constantly altering its geography and texture.

5
ASSOCIATIONS

The Multispecies City

Every metamorphosis is evidence of the relationship between disparate forms that defines the being of every living thing. This relationship is not something that lies outside our bodies. It is their very physiology. We are *both* caterpillar and butterfly. No silhouette, no ethos, no world can summarize our life. Every living being is the contraction and unfolding of an anatomical, ethical, ecological biodiversity, of which metamorphosis is the condition of possibility and the history.

From this point of view, a temporary association with other living beings, even a stable one, is no extra, accidental dimension of our life, another life added to our primary one in a second stage: it is rather the extension of our inner biodiversity, the amplification of the metamorphic force that animates us. The ecosystem and the city are spaces of metamorphic conspiracy, whirlpools where forms combine to make possible a greater metamorphosis of the Earth – that is, to impart to Gaia a more intense and richer life.

While the idea of the ecosystem has long been a device for slowing down and blocking metamorphosis, the human city was from the outset set up against the idea of life as an association of disparate forms, ethoses, and worlds. It has been a laboratory for the most radical form of ethical, ecological, and biological monoculture. Indeed, we tend to think of the city as an entirely mineral and therefore monospecies space: as a collection of human beings who live stably on a portion of Gaia's body, having manipulated the structure of this body to build their shelters. Everything that is neither mineral nor human – with very rare exceptions: cats, dogs, a few horses, ornamental plants and, illegally and clandestinely, rats and a few insects – is pushed back outside the city walls, into the forest – which already in its name (forest comes from the Latin *foris*, 'outside') is defined by a situation of lack: lack of civilization, lack of 'humanity', lack of modernity, lack of technology. This opposition, which has guided the way in which we have imagined our coexistence and our politics, is both illusory and dangerous. It is illusory because the creation of an opposition between the city or civilization and a so-called 'wild', 'natural' space is an entirely political myth, as William Cronon has brilliantly shown. The wild and the natural exist only for the city and for the human citizen: 'our own flight from "the city" creates "the wild" as its symbolic opposite and pulls that seemingly most natural of places into our own cultural orbit'.[1] The idea of natural space is, in a sense, the moral reversal of the political myth of a state of nature. For where modern political theory imagined the state as that which replaces a purely natural world, here the city seems to have to reconstruct a state of nature, a pre-political and wild world, in order to purify itself of the excesses of politics.

This tendency is also dangerous, because a space made only of stones is technically a desert, and the mineral fury of modern urbanism can only lead to the desertification of the planet. From this point of view, humanity, with its cities, seems to be the great Medusa of the planet. A mineral city operates in the opposite way to a forest. Every forest makes of life a force that allows the sunlight to collect in Gaia's body to bring her alive. For every plant, to grow is to accumulate light in its own body, to accumulate more and more light from an extra-terrestrial star. Every plant is therefore an agent for the assimilation of extra-terrestrial stellar matter into the mineral body of Gaia. The tree, which we imagine as the most terrestrial expression of life, contains and retains within its carbonic flesh a light that comes from elsewhere. An apple, a pear, a potato: little extra-terrestrial shards of light encapsulated in the mineral matter of our planet. It is this same light that each animal looks for in the body of the other when it eats (no matter whether it eats plants or other animals): every act of feeding is nothing other than a secret and invisible exchange of extra-terrestrial light which, through these movements, flows from body to body, from species to species, from kingdom to kingdom. Living beings transform stones into stellar deposits.

It is therefore unjust and inaccurate to accuse industrial farming of practising monoculture: cities are the real cradles of monoculture. It is at the moment when it is assumed that cohabitation with a different species can take place without any continuity or contact with others, that the illusion of an absolute life and of death as annihilation is produced. Cities nourish the illusion of the autonomy of the human body. From this point of view, they are funerary devices: they have enabled us to make the illusion of death symbolically true. All political science – as a discipline of human monoculture – is therefore radically compromised and must be abandoned. A purely human knowledge is not possible, because, as we have seen, all life (whether that of the individual or the species) is an interspecies affair. The science of living beings can only be a knowledge of interspecificity. On the other hand, we seem to have forgotten that any city presupposes a second body, a second interspecies Leviathan both agricultural and zootechnical, as its presupposition and condition of possibility, even if it has been condemned to live in exile outside the body of that city. No city can live without the interspecies encounter of women, men, plants, and animals that every meal celebrates and that every dwelling sanctifies: every city lives on the bodies of the plants and animals that are necessary to give life to the men and women who live there, to provide them with shelter, tools, furniture, energy, oxygen. Every human individual is only the daily reincarnation of all the chickens, salmon, cows, wheat, barley, and corn that it has eaten, digested, and transformed. Every artefact is the reincarnation of the labour and the bodies of other living beings, or of the mineral flesh of Gaia. The Leviathan whose life is the state is not simply composed of human bodies, but also and above all of all these animal and vegetable bodies, fungi, bacteria, and stones. It is they who donate all their power to the body 'politic'.

But realizing that any human community is part of an interspecies community means realizing that there is not, and should not be, any distinction between politics, agriculture, and animal husbandry. For there is nothing natural about a city. The form that a series of individuals gives to its own collective life always implies a project for the artificial modification of the lives of many other living beings. Interspecies association is only possible through interspecies metamorphosis. The coincidence between agriculture (and animal husbandry) and politics was still evident in the Platonic tradition (up until its overturning by Nietzsche) and in the biblical tradition, where politics was often compared to pastoral care. Modernity, on the contrary, draws from pastoral models only an abstract model of domination, leaving behind their most obvious element: the fact that the shepherd is of a different species from his flock.

If pastoralism and hunting, stockbreeding and agriculture are where all politics begin, it is not because the beginning of agriculture coincides with primitive accumulation. Pastoralism, hunting, and agriculture are the transcendental form of any possible politics, because no physical politics can be the internal affair of one single species. More generally, any association of individuals of the same species implies the conjoint association of individuals of other species and other kingdoms and their reciprocal metamorphosis. Not only is each city an interspecies association (and an inter-kingdom one: this is why agriculture is far more interesting than breeding or hunting), but every interspecies association is of a *technical* nature. On this second point our political and scientific tradition also needs to be improved: the technical relationship between two species is not purely and exclusively a human prerogative. The relationship of any species with other species is therefore a relationship of agriculture and husbandry: there is no natural relationship, because every species has *technical, artificial* relationships with other living species. It is by way of its technicality that the interspecies relationship induces the metamorphosis of the species entering into it. Agriculture, from this point of view, is something that happens on a cosmic scale – not just a question of the relationship between the human species and plant species, said to have arisen at a specific time and place in human history, but of the transcendental form of the relationship between all species, a relationship which in each case enables the genesis of the world. For the genesis of the world is a kind of interspecies relationship, not the emergence of a single individual from a single species. There is no world in which there is only one form of life. The world is always the result of cosmic agriculture or husbandry, of a metamorphic relationship between several species.

Interspecies Architecture

There is no natural environment. The world is always, in every part, conceived, designed, and built. And more importantly, space is always designed and built by other species, and for other species than the one that occupies it. This is why relations with the world are never simply physical or natural, but always political. For each species, being in the world means living in space designed and built by others. To live is therefore always to occupy, to invade a foreign space and to negotiate what a shared space could be.

Let's start with the most common, most trivial phenomenon relating to living beings (or at least animals): breathing. Our relationship to the world is first of all one of air and breath. For us, space is not only space to be travelled, seen, and touched. All living space must be breathable space. Space is therefore primarily the object of breathing, fuel for our lungs. And in this sense, the inaugural architectural act is not the construction of walls, but air-conditioning.

We are accustomed to thinking that breathing is the most natural of motions, the most obvious and ordinary relation connecting us to the world and to space. We are used to thinking of air as the most natural of elements, one that exists in its purest form, beyond any manipulation of nature. And yet air, with its 21% oxygen content, is only a by-product of plant life. It results from the metabolism of plants, it is the waste produced by their existence. In other words, it is an entity modified by someone, an artefact. The derivative of a plan, a project in the world, which does not come from humans or from individuals belonging to any species related to humans. Yet the result of this accidental, non-human conception makes the world viable for us. We know that the permanent settlement of animals on land was only made possible thanks to the radical metamorphosis of the layer of air that surrounds and envelops the Earth's crust, produced by plant invasion and the activity of cyanobacteria. Without the oxygen produced by photosynthesis, the Earth's atmosphere would not have changed its internal composition permanently and become the most immediate environment for all living things. From this point of view, the world is a plant entity far more than a zoological one, a garden rather than a zoo. And if the world is a garden, plants are not, or not really, or not only, the content of this garden or its inhabitants. They themselves are the gardeners. Recognizing this fact means that there is nothing transcendental or original about the Earth: it is an object produced by gardening. We, like all other animals, are the object of the gardening action of plants. We are one of their cultural and agricultural products. In more familiar terms, plants are not the content of the landscape but the very first landscapers. They metamorphose the world.

This very simple fact deserves to be considered more broadly as the paradigmatic example of the relationship between a species and space. It is not only plants that produce the face of our world, that shape and reshape the Earth: every living being does so. Architectural and urban agency is not something limited to the human being, it is the most widely shared faculty of living beings.

This is the conclusion to be drawn from the evidence of our animal nature: if mind is made up of atoms, tissues, and molecules, then mind is everywhere, in every living species. Biology is therefore a cosmic phenomenology of spirit. And reason expresses itself in non-human forms which we have both inherited and internalized.

Each species is a conscious actor, capable not only of mistakes and bad choices, but also of arbitrary behaviour that does not necessarily relate to what would be better and more useful for it. Every living species therefore also has an aesthetic relationship to the world around it.

Being alive does not just mean perceiving the world differently from other species, but also constructing it, shaping it in a different way. The environment is not something that pre-exists natural species, it is something that each species reshapes in its own image. The animate world is a world of architects. And because there is only one world and each species is in a sense obliged to live in a world produced and designed by others, and vice versa, architecture is always a multispecies affair.

So, humanity came into the world because the Earth had already been designed by other species . . . and not really for the good of humanity. To breathe is to use, to live off something that someone else has produced, and to turn that something into our first little cubbyhole. That's the goal. Space, or what we like to call the natural environment, is never 'natural'. What we call space is always a designed, produced space, not something that has been there, intact and equal to itself since the dawn of time. The space in which we live is the product of someone else. This architect of our common space (considered not only as a geometrical entity, but as a set of forms, objects, and contents of all kinds) is no man or woman or god. It is an individual (or group of individuals) belonging to another living species.

Since the world is the same for everyone and for all species, every act of design is also an act that blurs boundaries and disturbs the world of other species. Every time a bee, an oak tree, or a bacterium changes its environment to make its own life possible, this species also changes the environment of others. So architecture is not only the active relationship between a species and the world, but the necessary relationship between them. Each species relates to others as an architect of the world. Architecture is not just a human affair, a cultural fact. It is not even the relationship between a species and space, a form of life and its world. It is the paradigm of the interspecies relationship.

Our Mind is Always in the Bodies of Other Species

We are used to thinking that the interdependent relationships between different species are physical, energetic, or anatomical in nature. We never suspect that this interdependence is first of all of a cognitive and speculative order. If every relation between species is technical and artificial, not natural or purely physical, it is because every species finds its mind, its intelligence, its ability to think, *always* and *exclusively* in its relation with other species. Each species is linked to one or more other species as to its *mind*. This is the great lie of neurobiology: the intellect is not an organ, it always exists outside the body of every living individual.

Intellect is not a thing, it's a relation. It exists not in our body, but in the relations our body establishes with other bodies. If minds exist outside the body, it is because they are not the monospecific equipment of individuals: what we call mind is always an association between the life of two species. This idea of mind as ecology is not foreign to contemporary biology. The first to explore the idea was Paul Shepard in *Thinking Animals*,[2] where he showed how thinking is the effect, and not the condition of possibility, of the symbiotic cohabitation between plants, animals, bacteria, etc. It was only and always in interspecies relationships that large predators developed intelligence: without herbivores, large carnivorous predators would have been completely stupid. Shepard, however, still thought of this interspecificity of intelligence in teleological terms. On the contrary, we should imagine that the intellect of any species is embodied in another species.

You only have to look at a meadow to realize that. With the flower, the plant turns the insect into a geneticist, a breeder, a farmer: it entrusts another species belonging to another kingdom with the task of making a decision on the genetic and biological destiny of its own species. It entrusts them with the task of directing the metamorphosis of its species. In a certain sense, the flower transfers the plant's species-mind into the *body* of the bee. It is not simply a collaboration, it is the constitution of a cognitive and speculative interspecific organ. This means not only that all evolutionary development is co-evolution, as Peter Raven, Paul Ehrlich, and Donna Haraway have shown, but also that, as we have seen, co-evolution is what we normally call agriculture or husbandry. Each species decides, in its own way, the evolutionary fate of others. What we call evolution is nothing more than a kind of generalized interspecies agriculture, a cosmic crossbreeding – which is not necessarily designed for the benefit of one or the other. The world as a whole thus becomes a kind of purely relational reality where each species is the agro-ecological territory of the other: every living being is both garden and gardener of other species. The world then is this relation of reciprocal culture (never defined purely by the logic of utility, nor that of free usage). In this sense, no ecology is possible, because every ecosystem is the result of an agricultural practice and the involvement of other species. There is no wild space, just as there are no wild animals, because everything is cultivated. The relationship between culture and nature is always reversible: any species can embody nature for us, and vice versa.

The soil then ceases to be an autonomous reality.

There is no soil. The soil of one is the life of others. Politics can no longer be carried out on a territorial basis, but only on the basis of the interspecies relationship: so a city is only the relationship that a group of humans has with a series of other species (and with all the species that the existence of those species requires). There is no territory, no neutral space upon which the living could settle. Originary settlement is an act of agriculture or zootechnics. We always settle upon the lives of others, and, conversely, every one of us is always the soil for other living beings. Each lives off the body of the other. Each drew their body from the body of the other. As if, from the beginning, the Earth was a body formed of the bodies of all species, each of which lives off the lives of others, and all of which are inseparable.

Every living being is an Earth for others, every species is the terrain of life for an indefinite number of other actors, both living and non-living. There is no urban soil, no pure space to settle in, all is agricultural land. Soil is not what separates one living thing from another or one species from another, but what obliges each to mix with the other. Every territory is in itself a metamorphosis in progress, by virtue of which living beings, species, and non-living actors receive their share of the same power of acting that is common to the whole planet. Conversely, each of us, like all living things and all species, is part of a collective metamorphosis. A soil for other living things and other species. It is as the soil of others that we have a power to act.

This interspecies relationship that we call mind, intelligence, or 'brain' is not something natural. It is not spontaneous, eternal, purely biological – it is a technical fact and, in a sense, an artistic one. Any relationship between species must be read not only as something contingent, but as something like the relationship between an artist and the material they manipulate or, better still, as the relationship between a curator and an artist. The choice of insects as to which flower to mate with which other is not based on a rational calculation but on taste: how much sugar does the flower contain, that's the key. Evolution is therefore based on taste rather than utility. The sensitivities of one species decide the fate of other species. So evolution is just fashion in nature, a fashion show that lasts millions of years and allows any species to wear clothes taken from other species or that have been designed by others. Every landscape is an exhibition of contemporary nature or a masquerade where the fashions of nature are on display: a multispecies Biennial, an installation waiting to be replaced by hundreds of others.

Everything in nature, like everything in our own existence, is artificial and arbitrary. An artificiality produced by the action of different species. The history of the Earth is a history of art, an eternal artistic experiment. In this context, each species is both artist and curator of other species. And conversely, each species is both a work of art and a performance by the species whose evolution it represents, but also the object of an exhibition curated by those other species that made it emerge.

Evolution and natural selection are totally revolutionized. Fish, plants, lice, bacteria, viruses, fungi, and horses: whether large or extremely small, whatever kingdom they belong to, all living beings are minds, and not only for themselves (thinking, feeling, capable of decision-making), they are also the minds of other species. All living beings are capable not only of consciously changing their own and other species' environments, of forging arbitrary interspecies relationships that are not necessarily oriented towards some utility or other, but also of altering the destiny of other species. When looked at in this way, the world becomes the ever-changing result of this universal and cosmic intelligence and sensibility of the infinite forms of life. Conversely, this cosmic mind is produced by an infinite series of arbitrary and rational encounters and decisions taken by different species at different times, according to the strangest of intentions. Mind – that is to say, interspecies evolution – is the life of the metamorphosis of the world.

The End of Wilderness

Metamorphosis teaches us that being squirrel or boletus, kiwi fruit or dandelion, is not a destiny that has been assigned to us by an immortal subject and that we must accept as a natural given. The face of each species is an artefact, in the literal sense of the word: it is something that is built over time, using the most varied and disparate materials. Each species has built itself, following a series of arbitrary choices that are not necessarily related to needs imposed upon it by the environment. It was Darwin himself who suggested this explicitly. In 1871, in his book *The Descent of Man*, he realized that the morphological variety of many species could not be explained through the mere mechanism of natural selection – that is through a dynamism which is not controlled by living beings, and which 'obliges' them to adapt to the environment. The shapes of living bodies – their colours, decorative patterns, etc. – are not only expressions of the individual's adaptation to the world around them. They are also and above all the expression of a taste, of a sort of artistic will that drives the individual of a species to prefer one form over the other. With the term 'sexual selection' Darwin designated the fact that the evolution of species is also based on judgements of taste, actively expressed, almost always by female individuals. In 2017 the great ornithologist Richard Prum published an epochal study in which he confirmed and radicalized this intuition.[3] Species are nothing more than expressions of a 'biotic art', a sort of aesthetic performance conducted on an anatomical level. Ecology should stop mimicking economics or looking for a form of 'durability' – clearly an economic category. Instead, it should understand that all ecological problems are aesthetic problems in the sense in which, from Schiller onwards, this term has been used: to designate the sphere in which necessity and arbitrariness are combined in the alchemy that we call play. Species identity is therefore a space in which life ceaselessly plays with its own forms. And it is this game that we should begin to call architecture. Every species identity is a technical, architectural fact, and as such is never definitive, but remains subject to the changes which, generation upon generation, each individual will want to make to the building of which they are at once the structure, owner, inhabitant, and usufructuary. But if this is the case, then nothing in nature can any longer be considered as 'wild' or 'savage'.

Contemporary anthropology has long since enabled us to have done with the idea of the savage within the human world. What we imagined to be a radical cultural break turned out to be a difference in ways of articulating knowledge of the same object, the world, which nevertheless remain comparable in their 'intellectual application' and in their 'methods of observation'.[4] History can end up producing a considerable distance between cultures, sometimes greater than that caused by geography, but it can never break the continuity of human experience. On the other hand, there is no single modernity that we could oppose to a void, a lack of civilization and history – primitive time – but parallel and different forms of modernity which, moreover, have continually intersected and hybridized with one another. 'Modern' and 'scientific' thinking and 'wild' thinking are 'two parallel modes of acquiring knowledge [whose] theoretical and practical results differ in value [but which] require the same sort of mental operations and [. . .] differ not so much in kind as in the different types of phenomena to which they are applied'.[5] The attribute 'savage' is thus only the residue of the contempt and unthinking racism that any self-consciousness projects onto the foreigner: the presumption of superiority is an optical effect of any culture towards others. Every civilization tends to consider the other savage. 'When we make the mistake of thinking that the Savage is governed solely by organic or economic needs', wrote Claude Lévi-Strauss in his masterpiece *The Savage Mind*, 'we forget that he levels the same reproach at us, and that to him his own desires for knowledge seem more balanced than ours'.[6] It is not that some cultures are close to nature, nor that others are excessively mediated: there are just different formations of knowledge. Indeed, cultural difference can never be interpreted as a greater moral perfection: no culture gives us greater access to the Good than others.

Although the 'wild man' and the attribute of 'savageness' (along with that of the 'primitive') have now been excluded from historical and scientific discourse relating to different human cultures, similar tropes are still strongly present in the discourse around the non-human. We continue to speak of 'wild' spaces where living things construct a world without the contribution of the human species; we strive to define as 'wild' any form of life that is closer to its Good and to the conditions of possibility of its own maximum perfection.

The terms 'wild' and 'wilderness', when referring to non-human life, acquire a double meaning, as was well explained by William Cronon in a seminal essay that triggered an extremely broad and important debate.[7] According to Cronon, the history of this notion and the paradoxes it feeds are linked to neo-colonial and religious prejudices. On the one hand, the idea of savagery (wilderness) is nourished by the myth of the border, which presupposes that the American natural space was uninhabited and thus passes over in silence the massacre of local populations by colonists. On the other hand, the wilderness, previously considered negatively as a demonic place and the suspension of all forms of morality, has undergone a kind of sublimation that has transformed it into a place of encounter with divinity and thus of moral perfection. The myth of a wilderness that is expressed in the idea of a natural park is thus the inversion of the founding myth of the modern state. The latter thought of nature as what precedes the state and civilization: the association between human beings was supposed to replace, correct, and suspend the state of nature. The myth of 'wild' nature, on the contrary, sees the city fantasizing an outside self that would allow it to purify itself from the excesses of civilization and to balance them out. From this point of view, the attribute of wildness, when applied to non-human beings, fulfils a function opposite to the one it has when applied to human cultures: it does not belittle but instead exalts all that is supposedly devoid of culture and technics. Humanity may perhaps be considered technically superior, but morally inferior to other species. It is indeed because they lack reason and agility (and thus all forms of artifice and culture) that living things in the 'wild' state are supposedly 'purer' and more authentic than all human life: they are incapable of poor choices and errors, and are therefore unable to distance themselves from anything useful to them. It is because of its lack of subjectivity and freedom that the non-human being will never be able to distance itself from the Good. If, thanks to Darwin, biology has made it possible to understand that human life is no different from the life that is expressed in other life forms, it nevertheless continues to understand non-human life as being governed by an absolute and unfailing adherence to its own nature and its own perfection. There is nothing radically contingent about natural history: evolutionary choices made mechanically through competition necessarily produce local and global utility and promote the affirmation of the 'best' for the species as well as for their totality. It is impossible to imagine that non-human life can make bad choices. Impossible to imagine that there will be error, misunderstanding, catastrophes caused by the 'levity' of non-human species. There is a teleological order that allows all non-human life to automatically and unconsciously attain good and perfection.

The logic of utility implied in evolution is thus seen to represent a more acute form of rationality than any human doctrine, allowing non-human communities to do without any form of civilization, any accumulated and transmitted knowledge, any historical contingency. It is this theological bias (for it is impossible to demonstrate scientifically that non-human life tends by itself to its own good and that evolution always makes choices beneficial to species) that makes it possible to think of the 'wild' as a more morally perfect order than the political order produced within humanity and the world of artifice, which often leads to error.

To overcome this prejudice – to have done with savagery and the wild – it is therefore not enough to affirm that man is an animal species: it is necessary to put a stop to the impulse to idealization that afflicts both human life and non-human life, placing them in moral opposition. Everything that constitutes us derives from the non-human and has the same nature, but the reverse is also true: everything that defines humanity, beginning with error, art, artifice, and moral arbitration, also defines the totality of living species. The consequence that a post-Darwinian biology should be able to draw from this fact is that there is a perfect equivalence between all species not only from an ontological or a cognitive point of view, but also from a moral point of view. All species in nature are morally equivalent. And all species are ambivalent: they do not automatically tend towards the Good, they do not always do the right thing. Every species, because of its freedom, can also make bad choices, for itself and for nature in general.

If the mind is a matter of atoms, tissues, and molecules, then it is everywhere, in every living species, even if in different forms; and inversely, in a world where every form of life has a mind, a mind capable of error, no species can be considered either exemplary or scandalous. All life and all ethoses are cultural facts, everything is artificial, everything is also arbitrary, contingent, and sometimes dark, enigmatic, equivocal, as it is for humans. Biology should be transformed into a phenomenology of the cosmic mind, which would show how reason expresses itself mainly through non-human forms, which we have both inherited and internalized. And this phenomenology will not always be a day trip to paradise.

Contemporary Nature

Each species decides the evolutionary destiny of the other, at once artist and work. We humans, for example, are a work of art made by those primates who decided to modify their bodies to produce another way of life. We are a species-performance by them that has lasted for three hundred thousand years.

The Earth itself must be considered as an artistic experiment. Evolution is in fact the production of what should be called contemporary nature.

From the beginning of the twentieth century, when art established itself as avant-garde, it ceased to fulfil an aesthetic function. It freed itself from the task of producing beauty, of decorating what already exists and bringing it into harmony. In claiming to be contemporary – that is, in claiming to embody a form of time and not a form of space or matter – art became a collective practice of the divination of the future. From that moment on, through art, every society constructs something that does not yet exist within it: no longer a harmonious reflection of its own nature, but an attempt to reproduce itself differently from what it is, a way of being different and of divining a difference that does not yet exist. Art embodies a society's desire for and project of metamorphosis.

Contemporary art is not defined by any particular medium, method, or discipline: it is a movement that crosses over and disrupts all media, all cultural practices and all cultural disciplines, so as to allow culture to differentiate itself from what it is. Art is the space in which a society manages to render visible what it cannot confess, think, or imagine.

We should think of evolution as the mode of life that corresponds to what contemporary art is for culture. Nature is not only the immemorial prehistory of culture, but its unrealized future; its surrealistic anticipation. Contemporary nature is the scene where life enters into the avant-garde of its future. It is life as a natural avant-garde. It is the surrealistic reproduction of forms of life.

Cities should become something like museums for contemporary nature, not just ecosystems of cohabitation. The concept of the ecosystem continues to presuppose the idea of a natural and immutable equilibrium in which any human intervention is perturbing and which excludes all technical innovation. What we have said about evolution as technical progress should be enough to convince us that every ecosystem is in fact a city – i.e., a space where innovation and progress are concentrated – and a museum of contemporary nature, a space where this progress does not follow a predetermined logic, but is freely available to all species.

The city as a museum of contemporary nature is nothing other than a collection of arts and technics in perfect continuity with our own. It will contain a kind of hybrid of old museums, zoos or botanical gardens, old human cities and white cubes. Life in these institutions will have to coincide with a kind of interspecies urban planning, a multispecies landscape architecture.

These new museums will have to be the promoters of an 'eco-surrealist' (but not necessarily eco-modernist) culture, capable of imagining nature beyond its limits. Bringing together artists, scientists, designers, architects, and farmers, it will be a matter of building multispecies associations somewhere between city, garden, plantation, and stable, where each living being produces works for others and for themselves. In this virtuous exercise of the imagination, both aesthetically and naturally, cities become the practice of a collective metamorphosis of species.

The city must become what makes the contemporaneity of nature possible. Nature is not the prehistory of civilization. It is our present and above all our future. It is always a futuristic projection of the present – its metamorphosis.

CONCLUSION

Planetary Knowledge

One of the greatest contemporary Amazonian thinkers, Ailton Krenak, often says that life is not something around us, but something that flows through us from both inside and out. There is no environment – nor any environing life – but only a flow, a continuum of which we are a metamorphic action.

I have tried to show that metamorphosis is the evidence that all the life that exists around and outside us is the same as the life that lies within us, and vice versa. We live the same life as everything around us. This is what we discovered when, for the first time, we noticed the cocoon by means of which a caterpillar transforms into a butterfly. One and the same life shared by two bodies – two bodies that have nothing in common from an anatomical, ethological, or ecological point of view: they have totally different forms and lives. As we saw, the insect is a schizophrenic life divided between two bodies, the first consisting of an enormous digestive tract on a kind of six-legged tank that does nothing but eat, the second a flying machine that spends its time sexually coupling with individuals of the same species. Metamorphosis is just the mechanism that allows these two incompatible bodies to belong to the same individual. These two bodies inhabit two completely different worlds: the first crawls on the ground, the second lives in the air. The miracle of metamorphosis is therefore that of a shared life which cannot be traced back to a precise anatomical identity or a specific world. The same self, the same 'I', can live in two incompatible bodies and two incompatible worlds. As if we were to spend half of our lives with six legs, living by clinging to the ground and eating leaves, and the other half of our lives hovering in the air making love every two hours. This would prevent us from ever considering our life as the property of any specific form of body or world. Life for us would be what passes between bodies, what can circulate between different worlds, not a fixed and specific quality.

Metamorphosis is this miracle: two bodies, but the same life. We usually think that two bodies of different forms have nothing in common, but they have the same life, they are the same self, they have the same relationship that we have with our own child's body. What I wanted to show in this book is that this relationship is not limited to the caterpillar and the butterfly, but exists between all the bodies in the world, and between all living bodies and the Earth. The very same life that animates us ceaselessly modifies bodies, exploiting matter to change its clothes, to shape Gaia's body differently. Take all living beings, not just those that belong to a species, but those belonging to all species; not only those alive now, but all those that have lived since life began and those that will live in the future. They have the same relationship to each other as the caterpillar and the butterfly. They consist of the same life, transmitted from one body to another, from one species to another. The same applies to the living being and the Earth: life is only the butterfly of this huge caterpillar that is Gaia, it is the metamorphosis of the planet.

As I have tried to show, this continuity applies first of all on an intraspecies level, through birth, but also on a physiological and evolutionary level. For any species identity first of all defines a formula for continuity (and metamorphosis) with other species. On this point, Darwinism, if read consistently and radically enough, could coincide with what has been highlighted by contemporary anthropology in the analyses of Eduardo Viveiros de Castro.[1] If any relationship between individuals of the same species is isomorphic with the relationship between different species, if there is a perfect analogy between the birth cycle of individuals and the genesis of the species, if there is a perfect analogy between the cycle of birth and the genesis of a new species, then the taxonomy of species cannot be considered as a natural fact, but must be seen as one of the kinship patterns that allow us to classify human cultures. The relationship between living beings is a cultural form of kinship that must be constantly renegotiated, just as our kinship relationships have to be shaped and negotiated.

The perspective developed above suggests a series of conclusions both epistemological and political. If every species is intrinsically interspecific, contrary to what has been believed and repeated for centuries, all knowledge, all science, at every moment of its development, at every geographical and cultural stage, is a form of totemism. We might say that it is always by observing the nonhuman that mankind (and any other species) has been and will be able to understand itself: all knowledge concerning our lives can only be drawn from observation. Self-consciousness is always an interspecies affair. It is by applying to them concepts that describe our life that we have understood the life of species and life forms different from our own. Totemism and anthropomorphism, from this point of view, are one and the same process: if we discover that a part of our life is identical to that of non-humans, we also recognize features of humanity in the latter; conversely, each time we attribute a human trait to a plant or an animal, we also recognize that there is something within us that is not exclusively human. And both of these processes are structurally necessary: if each species is defined as a minimal modification of a species that preceded it, then any knowledge of a single species is constitutively interspecific. From a certain point of view, all knowledge is totemic because there can be no knowledge that is not borrowed from other living beings. And vice versa, all self-knowledge is always knowledge of other life forms, because each life form is a collage of many species.

Future

For centuries we have been scanning the skies for signs to help us divine the future. We looked up and imagined that we could see what was to come by observing the shifting and varying geometries that other bodies – the stars – seemed to mark out upon its ethereal body. That is why the science of the future or the vernacular knowledge of what is to come is still called 'astrology': the science of celestial bodies. For centuries we have observed, worshipped, and venerated parts of the sky, the stars, or rather their luminous image in that part of the sky we see every night, as the cause of all that happens to us and will happen to us.

This belief has been consistently accompanied by another. For centuries, we have considered the Earth to be the most sacred guardian of our past. It is to the Earth that we have always entrusted our dead. It is the Earth and the ruins that spill out of its womb that we have always asked to tell us what we have been. For centuries we have considered the Earth as a pure effect, a mere cosmic repository of everything that happened elsewhere, the junkyard of the human and non-human universe. A mass of ruins.

For centuries, and for reasons that are not easily summarized, we have been victims of this strange parallax error that has made us confuse the future and the past, the sky with what we believed to be its opposite.

We must correct this error of vision and build an inverted astrology: a true science of the future that knows where to look. We must understand where the future lies, and the manner in which it exists.

Astrology needs to be reversed for at least three reasons. Firstly, because we know today that everything that appears in the sky happened many years ago – often millions of years ago. Not only is there no future in the sky, there is no longer any trace of the present. The distant images of the sky are just ruins – preserved in formaldehyde for a few million years in order to be viewed. The firmament is the largest archaeological site in the cosmos, a huge open-air museum capable of bringing to life the past of the universe in the form of a spectacle that circulates from planet to planet. The astrological heavens are the travelling circus of the past of the cosmos.

But if astrology needs to be turned upside down, it is also because we know that the Earth itself is a celestial body. The sky and everything to be found between our atmosphere and the Sun have the same substance, the same matter, the same form as the Earth: we are the sky by nature, by matter, by form.

Astrology must therefore learn to be an Earth science. And to achieve this we must understand that, if we want to know the future, we must look not up but down, and turn towards this bit of sky that is our own planet. In fact, everything that appears on Earth is a future anticipated in the form of a wager. Every body on Earth is a hedge fund. The Earth is itself a future body and a futuristic body – the future of all bodies. This is what we must learn. We must not respect the Earth for its fragility. We must experience it differently, because the planet is our future flesh. The flesh of tomorrow, of the day after tomorrow and of a thousand million years to come.

The fact that the Earth is our future means that the future never comes from outside. On the contrary, if there is a future it is only because there is no exteriority, because everything is already inside. Inside this planet. Everything on its surface. The future is the skin of the planet, which is undergoing continual transformation: it is the cocoon of its metamorphosis.

The Earth is the body of the future not because of its size – the future is never something big, something immense. It is not a meteor that threatens to destroy the mass of the planet. It belongs to it as something smaller than the smallest of its inhabitants. The future is closer to the way in which viruses live than to humans or their monuments. The future is absolutely microscopic. From the perspective of the future, life exists even in the smallest portion of matter.

A virus, we might say, simplifying somewhat, is like the chemical, material, dynamic mechanism of development and reproduction of all living beings, but existing outside the cell structure in a more anarchic, freer form. It could be said that the virus is the force that allows each body to develop its own form, as if it existed disincarnated from the body, liberated, free-floating, as a pure power of metamorphosis. This is what the future is, a force for the development and reproduction of life which does not belong to us, which is not the exclusive property of an individual, and is not even common and shared, but is rather a power floating on the surface of all other bodies. Precisely because it is free, this force circulates from body to body. It is available to all, capable of being appropriated by each and every one of them. But just as appropriating a virus means contaminating oneself, transforming oneself, metamorphosing oneself, so appropriating the future means exposing oneself to irreparable change.

The future is the pure force of metamorphosis, capable of existing not only as the tendency of an individual body but as an autonomous body, like pollen flying through the air: an infinitely appropriable resource. The future is the fact that life and its force are everywhere and cannot belong to any of us, either as individuals, as a nation, or as a species. The future is a disease that obliges individuals and populations alike to change. A disease that prevents us from thinking of our identity as something stable, definitive, or real.

The future, after all, is the disease of eternity. A singular tumour. But a benign one. The only one that makes us better.

We don't need to protect ourselves from this disease. We don't need to vaccinate ourselves against the virus of time. There's no point. Our flesh will never stop changing. We need to be sick, very sick. Unafraid of dying. We are the future. We live fast. We die often.

Bibliography

In the lineage of living beings, no one occupies the position of Adam. In the sequence of words, none can really be considered as the one that preceded all others. There is never a true beginning in language: every word is an echo of what preceded it and an anticipation of what follows it. This book extends and transforms ideas that come from elsewhere: it is both their cocoon and their metamorphosis.

In addition to the dialogues with friends who have accompanied me, in addition to that silent dialogue with the world that we call experience, other words, other works, and other books have made possible the writing of this text. Given the breadth of the questions addressed, the work involved a great deal of reading over several years: without providing a detailed list, I will limit myself to naming the works that were the most significant in imagining this book. Foremost among them, and far more than what appears in the lines of Book XV of Ovid's *Metamorphoses*, a masterpiece neglected by philosophy: from the mouth of Pythagoras there emerges a metaphysics of reincarnation and of the drifting of the flesh and the spirit that enabled Ovid to write some of the most radical and visionary pages ever written.

The book then attempts to develop and radicalize the proposition put forward by James Lovelock and Lynn Margulis in the Gaia hypothesis.

Births

Birth remains a taboo in the contemporary system of knowledge. Apart from in obstetrics and astrology, very little is said or written outside pop psychology about the feelings which the mother feels 'naturally' for her children. This is why the inspiration for this chapter comes, more than from written sources, from a visit to Kiki Smith's sublime exhibition 'Processions' at the Haus der Kunst in Munich, which opened in February 2018 and was organized by Petra Giloy-Hirtz, in particular the works *Rapture* (2001) and *Born* (2002) in which the female figure emerges from the womb of a wolf and a young deer: our origin is non-human, and our kinship with all living species coincides with the sharing of the same flesh that has been transmitted from one living being to another since the Big Bang. The miracle and the violence of every birth is captured here in an extremely striking way.

Some works in German – including Christina Schües, *Philosophy des Geborenseins* (Freiburg and Munich: Verlag Karl Alber, 2008), and Ludger Lütkehaus, *Natalität. Philosophie der Geburt* (Zug: Die Graue Edition, 2006) – have attempted to trace the hidden and intermittent history of this theme in European philosophy.

One of the many reasons for this vacuum is also the monopolization of the discourse on birth by Christian theology. As proof one need only look at the apocryphal literature around the divine birth. On this subject, it is essential to consult the volume by J.K. Elliott, *A Synopsis of the Apocryphal Nativity and Infancy Narratives* (Leiden and Boston: E.J. Brill, 2006). Of all the Christian treatises on the nativity of Christ, the one that has left the greatest impression on me was that of Paschasius Radbertus, the nineteenth-century theologian who composed *De partu virginis*, edited by E.A. Matter and A. Ripberger (Turnhout: Corpus Christianorum, Continuatio mediaevalis, LVI C, 1985). Hannah Arendt's pages on the subject of birth, in *The Human Condition* (Chicago: University of Chicago Press, 1998), can be traced back to this myth. On Arendt, see also Patricia Bowen-Moore's essay, *Hannah Arendt's Philosophy of Natality* (London: Macmillan Press, 1989). Theology has been the source of extremely significant iconographic reflection on birth, the subject of a masterly study by Giulia Puma, *Les nativités italiennes (1250–1450). Une histoire d'adoration* (Rome: École française de Rome, 2019). The overthrow of the Christian theology of birth proposed in the book is approached on the basis of Samuel Butler's masterpiece, *God the Known and God the Unknown* (London: A.C. Fifield, 2009).

The paragraph on Ferenczi was drawn from the volume *Thalassa: A Theory of Genitality*, translated by Henry Alden Bunker (New York: Norton, 1968).

Cocoons

The literature I have consulted on metamorphosis is extremely vast. I have tried to summarize as concisely as possible some of a debate that has been going on since the sixteenth century. The first important modern text is that of Thomas Moffet, *Insectorum sive minimorum animalium theatrum* (London: Thomas Cotes, 1634), followed by the works of William Harvey, *Exercitationes de generation animalium, Apud Joannem Janssonium* (Amsterdam, 1651), then by Johannes Goedart's 1658 *Metamorphosis Naturalis* (English translation by Francis Place and Martin Lister, *Of Insects* [York: John White, 1682]), and by Jan Swammerdam, *Biblia naturæ: sive, Historia insectorum in classes certas redacta*, trans. Hieronimus David Gaubius (Leiden, 1737).

The phrase about the schizophrenic body of insects is taken from Carroll M. Williams's masterful essay 'Hormonal Regulation of Insect Metamorphosis', in W.D. McElroy and B. Glass (eds.), *Symposium on the Chemical Basis of Development* (Baltimore: Johns Hopkins University Press, 1958), pp. 794–806. See also his 'Morphogenesis and Metamorphosis of Insects', *Harvey Lectures* 47 (1951–52), pp. 126–55.

The complete bibliography on contemporary research on insect metamorphosis is immense. It would be impossible to summarize it here. A very detailed historical panorama has been compiled by Deniz F. Erezyilmaz, 'Imperfect Eggs and Oviform Nymphs: A History of Ideas about the Origins of Insect Metamorphosis', *Integrative and Comparative Biology* 46:6, pp. 795–807. By the same author, see Deniz F. Erezyilmaz, Lynn M. Riddiford, and James W. Truman, 'The Pupal Specifier Broad Directs Progressive Morphogenesis in a Direct Developing', *Insect. Proc Natl Acad Sci USA* 103 (2006), pp. 6925–30. Important historical and theoretical syntheses include the essay by James W. Truman and Lynn M. Riddiford, 'The Origins of Insect Metamorphosis', *Nature* 410 (1999), pp. 447–52; and Aniruddha Mitra, 'Cinderella's New Shoes: How and Why Insects Remodel Their Bodies Between Life Stages', in *Current Science* 104 (2013), pp. 1028–36.

Among the many historical articles consulted, the most important for composing this book was the text by Antonio Berlese, an Italian entomologist who first defended the thesis of de-embryonization in 'Intorno alle metamorfosi degli insetti', *Redia* 9 (1913), pp. 121–36; H. Henson, 'The Theoretical Aspect of Insect Metamorphosis', *Biological Review* 21 (1946), pp. 1–14; and H.E. Hinton, 'On the Origin and Function of the Pupal Stage', *Transactions of the Royal Entomological Society of London* 99 (1948), pp. 395–409. The work of Vincent B. Wigglesworth was also decisive, including *The Physiology of Insect Metamorphosis* (Cambridge: Cambridge University Press, 1954); I also profited greatly from reading his *Insects and the Life of Man: Collected Essays on Pure Science and Applied Biology* (London: Chapman & Hall, 1976).

See also the fine book by Frank Ryan, *Metamorphosis: Unmasking the Mystery of How Life Transforms* (London: Oneworld Publications, 2012). And by Donald Irving Williamson, apart from his book *The Origins of Larvae* (Norwell: Kluwer Academic Publishers, 2003), his articles and contributions to collections are most important, including 'Sequential Chimeras', in A.I. Tauber (ed.), *Organism and the Origins of Self* (Dordrecht: Kluwer, 1991), pp. 299–336; 'Larval Transfer in Evolution', in M. Syvanen and C.I. Kado (eds.), *Horizontal Gene Transfer* (New York: Academic Press, 2001), pp. 395–410; 'Larval Transfer and the Origins of Larvae', *Zoological Journal of the Linnean Society* 131:1 (2001), pp. 111–22; 'Hybridization in the Evolution of Animal Form and Life-Cycle', *Zoological Journal of the Linnean Society* 148:4 (2006), pp. 585–602; 'Caterpillars Evolved from Onychophorans by Hybridogenesis', *Proceedings of the National Academy of Sciences of the USA* 106 (2009), pp. 19901–5;

'Larval Genome Transfer: Hybridogenesis in Animal Phylogeny', at http://retractionwatch.files.wordpress.com/2011/10/diw_2011_symbiosis.pdf.

On Maria Sibylla Merian, I consulted two recent studies: Kurt Wettengl (ed.), *Maria Sibylla Merian. Künstlerin und Naturforscherin 1647–1717* (Berlin: Hatje Cantz Verlag, 2013); and Carin Grabowski (ed.), *Maria Sibylla Merian zwischen Malerei und Naturforschung: Pflanzen- und Schmetterlingsbilder Neu Entdeckt* (Berlin: Dietrich Reimer, 2017).

On the more general theoretical issues raised in these chapters, the works of John T. Bonner, a biologist in the Department of Ecology and Evolutionary Biology at Princeton University, were decisive. Among his many books are *Size and Cycle: An Essay on the Structure of Biology* (Princeton: Princeton University Press, 1966); *On Development: The Biology of Form* (Cambridge, MA: Harvard University Press, 1974); and *First Signals: The Evolution of Multicellular Development* (Princeton: Princeton University Press, 2001). On the question of rejuvenation, see Alexander Braun, botanist, Director of the Berlin Botanical Garden and teacher of Ernst Haeckel, *Betrachtungen über die Erscheinung der Verjüngung in der Natur* (Leipzig: Verlag von Wilhelm Engelmann, 1851); and Ruth G. Rinard's article 'The Problem of the Organic Individual: Ernst Haeckel and the Development of the Biogenetic Law', *Journal of the History of Biology* 14 (1981), pp. 249–75.

On the jellyfish *Turritopsis nutricula*, see Stefano Piraino, Ferdinando Boero, Brigitte Aeschbach, and Volker Schmid, 'Reversing the Life Cycle: Medusae Transforming into Polyps and Cell Transdifferentiation in *Turritopsis nutricula* (Cnidaria, Hydrozoa)', *Biological Bulletin* 190 (1996), pp. 302–12.

Ernst Kapp's masterpiece has been translated into

English as *Elements of a Philosophy of Technology*, translated by Lauren K. Wolfe (Minneapolis: Minnesota University Press, 2018).

On the debate concerning the metamorphosis of plants, Johann Wolfgang von Goethe's *The Metamorphosis of Plants* (Cambridge, MA: MIT Press, 2009) enters into dialogue with Carl Linnaeus's *Philosophia Botanica*, translated by Stephen Freer (Oxford: Oxford University Press, 2003); the text by Nils Ericsson Dahlberg, *Metamorphosis plantarum* (1755); and Caspar Friedrich Wolff's work 'De formatione intestinorum praecipue, tum et de amnio spurio aliisque partibus embryonis gallinacei, nondum visis, observationes in ovis incubatis institutae', in *Novi Commentarii Academiae Scientiarum Imperialis Petropolitanae* (Petropoli Typis Academiae Scientiarum, 20 vols, 1747–75), vol. 12, pp. 403–507, vol. 13, pp. 478–530.

Reincarnations

I developed the idea of reincarnation by way of reflections on the art of Philippe Parreno.

Val Plumwood has recounted her expedition several times. The final version is contained in the posthumous collection *The Eye of the Crocodile*, edited by Lorraine Shannon (Canberra: Australian National University E-Press, 2012).

On the question of resurrection, the literature is immense, especially following Oscar Cullmann's famous book *Unsterblichkeit der Seele oder Auferstehung der Toten* (Stuttgart: Kreuz, 1967), which underlined the difference between the thesis of the immortality of the soul and that of the resurrection of the body. Alan F. Segal's classic *Life After Death: A History of the Afterlife in the Religion of the West* (New York: Doubleday, 2004), and

Candida R. Moss's recent *Divine Bodies: Resurrecting Perfection in the New Testament and Early Christianity* (New Haven: Yale University Press, 2019) supply some orientation. Aldo Leopold's 'Odyssey' is contained in his posthumous collection, *A Sand County Almanac and Sketches Here and There* (Oxford: Oxford University Press, 1949). On Leopold, see Julianne Lutz Warren's study, *Aldo Leopold's Odyssey: Rediscovering the Author of a Sand County Almanac* (Washington: Island Press, 2016).

On sexuality from a biological perspective, see Lynn Margulis and Dorian Sagan's masterpiece, *What is Life? Three Million Years of Genetic Reconstruction* (New Haven: Yale University Press, 1990).

On the discovery of the alternation of generations, two essays give some orientation: Armin Geus, 'Der Generationswechsel: Die Geschichte eines biologischen Problems', *Medizinhistorisches Journal* 7 (1972), pp. 159–73, and Dieter Zissler, 'Die Entdeckungsgeschichte des Generationswechsel der Tiere', *Mitteilungen des Badischen Landesvereins für Naturkunde und Naturschutz e.V. Freiburg i. Br.* (2001), pp. 951–66.

Adelbert von Chamisso's book *De animalibus quibusdam e classe vermium Linnaeana in circumnavigatione Terrae: De Salpa* (Berlin: F. Dümmler, 1819) opened up a discussion with, among others, M. Sars, *Bidrag til Söedyrenes Naturhistorie* (Bergen, 1829), and J.J.S. Steenstrup, *Ueber den Generationswechsel oder die Fortpflanzung und Entwickelung durch abwechselnde Métamorphoses Generationen, eine eigenthümliche Form der Brutpflege in den niederen Thierclassen* (Copenhagen, 1842). Chamisso's voyage of discovery was recounted by the author in 'Voyage de Kotzebue. Lettre écrite à M. le Comte de Romanzoff, par M. de Chamisso naturaliste français, qui a fait le voyage autour du monde, avec M. de Kotzebue, sur le brick russe le *Rurik*', *Journal des voyages découvertes et navigations modernes; ou Archives géographiques et statitiques du xixe siècle* (Paris, 1821), pp. 201–8.

On all these questions, the line of thought developed in Leo W. Buss's *The Evolution of Individuality* (Princeton: Princeton University Press, 1987) is absolutely essential.

Migrations

Part of the text was written as a commentary on the work of Christine Rebet.

Alfred Wegener's masterpiece has been published in its first and fourth edition with his handwritten notes, *Die Entstehung der Kontinente und Ozeane, Gebrüder Borntraeger Verlagsbuchhandlung* (Berlin, 2015). On plate tectonics see the classic history by Henry R. Frankel, *The Continental Drift Controversy* (Cambridge: Cambridge University Press, 4 vols, 2012); and more recently, Roy Livermore, *The Tectonic Plates are Moving!* (Oxford: Oxford University Press, 2018).

On the history of ecology, there is a very good introduction in French by Jean-Paul Deléage, *Histoire de l'écologie* (Paris: La Découverte, 1991), in addition to the volumes by Ludwig Trepl, *Geschichte der Ökologie. Vom 17, Jahrhundert bis zur Gegenwart* (Frankfurt am Main: Athenäeum, 1987), and Frank N. Egerton, *Roots of Ecology: Antiquity to Haeckel* (Berkeley: University of California Press, 2012). The texts of Linnaeus and his students can be read in French in the volume Carl von Linnaeus, *L'Équilibre de la nature*, translated by Bernard Jasmin (Paris: Vrin, 1972).

Henri Lecoq published his *Étude de la géographie botanique de l'Europe* (Paris: Baillière et Fils) in eight volumes, from 1854 to 1858.

On the ecology of invasion, see Charles Elton's book *The Ecology of Invasions by Animals and Plants* (London: Methuen, 1958). As for the reaction this book triggered, there is a collection edited by David M. Richardson, *Fifty Years of Invasion Ecology: The Legacy of Charles Elton* (Chichester: Wiley Blackwell, 2011); and a very important book by Jacques Tassin, *La Grande Invasion* (Paris: Odile Jacob, 2014).

Hewlett C. Watson published his *Remarks on the Geographical Distribution of British Plants, Chiefly in Connection with Latitude, Elevation, and Climate*, with Longman in London in 1835. His *Cybele Britannica* was published, also by Longman, from 1847.

On plant migration, see Gilles Clément, *Le Jardin planétaire. Réconcilier l'homme et la nature* (Paris: Albin Michel, 1999), and Stefano Mancuso, *L'Incredibile Viaggio della piante* (Rome: Laterza, 2018).

Associations

Apart from William Cronon's book *Nature's Metropolis: Chicago and the Great West* (New York: W.W. Norton, 1991), and Carolyn Steel's *Hungry City: How Food Shapes Our Lives* (London: Penguin, 2013), this chapter was inspired by Philippe Parreno's 2011 film *Continuously Habitable Zones a.k.a. CHZ*, made in collaboration with Bas Smets, and by Pierre Huyghe's sculpture *Exomind*, created in 2017.

The book by Paul Shepard cited is *Thinking Animals: Animals and the Development of Human Intelligence* (Atlanta: University of Georgia Press, 1998).

The closing vision of a museum for contemporary

nature owes much to Stefano Boeri's *Vertical Forest* (2015) in Milan.

Conclusion

The words of Ailton Krenak are drawn from *Ideas to Postpone the End of the World*, translated by Anthony Doyle (Toronto: House of Anansi Press, 2020).

For Eduardo Viveiros de Castro, see *Cannibal Metaphysics: For a Post-Structural Anthropology*, translated by Peter Skafish (Minneapolis: Univocal, 2014).

Notes

1 BIRTHS

1 'The Latin Infancy Gospels', in Bart D. Ehrman and Zlatko Pleše, *The Apocryphal Gospels: Texts and Translations* (Oxford: Oxford University Press, 2011), p. 127.
2 Ibid.
3 Hannah Arendt, *The Life of the Mind* (San Diego: Harcourt, 1978), p. 212.
4 Hannah Arendt, *The Human Condition* (Chicago: University of Chicago Press, 1998), p. 177.
5 Ibid.
6 Hannah Arendt, *Crises of the Republic* (San Diego: Harcourt, 1972), p. 179.
7 Samuel Butler, *God the Known and God the Unknown* (London: A.C. Fifield, 1909), p. 69.
8 Ibid.
9 Ibid., p. 62.
10 Sándor Ferenczi, *Thalassa: A Theory of Genitality*, trans. Henry Alden Bunker (New York: Norton, 1968), p. 45.
11 Ibid., p. 62.
12 Ibid., p. 66.

13 Ibid., p. 50.
14 Ibid., p. 54.

2 COCOONS

1 Jan Godard (Johannes Goedartius), *Metamorphosis et historia naturalis insectorum. Autore Joanne Goedartio. Cum commentariis d. Joannis de Mey...* (Middelburg, 1662), pp. 4–5.
2 Voltaire, *The Philosophical Dictionary of M. Voltaire* (New York: George H. Evans, 1835), pp. 162–3.
3 Jan Swammerdam, *The Book of Nature, or, The History of Insects*, trans. Thomas Flloyd and John Hill (London: C.G. Seyffert, 1758), p. 3.
4 Ibid., p. 9.
5 Ibid., p. 10.
6 Maria Sibylla Merian, Foreword to *Metamorphosis insectorum Surinamensium* (1705).
7 Maria Sibylla Merian, *Caterpillars* (1679), quoted in Donna Spalding Andréolle and Véronique Molinari (eds.), *Women and Science, 17th Century to Present: Pioneers, Activists and Protagonists* (Cambridge: Cambridge Scholars Publishing, 2011), p. 39.
8 Donald I. Williamson, *The Origins of Larvae* (New York: Springer, 2003), p. 1.
9 Donald I. Williamson, 'Introduction to Larval Transfer', *Cell & Developmental Biology* 1:5 (2012), p. 1.
10 Donald I. Williamson, 'Sequential Chimeras', in Alfred I. Tauber (ed.), *Organism and the Origins of Self* (Dordrecht: Kluwer, 1991), p. 299.
11 Ibid., p. 334.
12 Ibid., p. 299.
13 Donald I. Williamson, 'Caterpillars Evolved from Onychophorans by Hybridogenesis', *PNAS* 106:47 (2009), 19901–5, p. 19903.

14 Ibid., p. 19903.
15 Donald I. Williamson, 'Hybridization in the Evolution of Animal Form and Life-Cycle', *Zoological Journal of the Linnean Society* 148:4 (2006), 585–602, p. 586.
16 Williamson, 'Sequential Chimeras', p. 303.
17 Carroll M. Williams, 'Hormonal Regulation of Insect Metamorphosis', in W.D. McElroy and B. Glass (eds.), *Symposium on the Chemical Basis of Development* (Baltimore: Johns Hopkins University Press, 1958), 794–806, p. 794.
18 William Harvey, 'On Generation', in *The Works of William Harvey*, trans. Robert Willis (London: Sydenham Society, 1847), p. 457.
19 Aristotle, *Generation of Animals*, trans. A.I. Peck (London and Cambridge, MA: Loeb, 1943), p. 329.
20 Antonio Berlese, 'Intorno alle metamorfosi degli insetti', *Redia* 9 (1913), p. 126.
21 Harvey, 'On Generation', p. 459.
22 Ibid.
23 H. Henson, 'The Theoretical Aspect of Insect Metamorphosis', *Biological Reviews* 21:1 (January 1946), 1–14, p. 1.
24 Ibid., p. 13.
25 Harvey, 'On Generation', p. 271.
26 Ibid.
27 Alexander Braun, 'Reflections on the Phenomenon of Rejuvenescence in Nature, Especially in the Life and Development of Plants', trans. A. Henfrey, in *Botanical and Physiological Memoirs* (London: The Ray Society, 1853), p. 2.
28 Ibid.
29 Ibid., p. 3.
30 Ibid.
31 Ibid.

32 Stefano Piraino, Ferdinando Boero, Brigitte Aeschbach, and Volker Schmid, 'Reversing the Life Cycle: Medusae Transforming into Polyps and Cell Transdifferentiation in *Turritopsis nutricula* (Cnidaria, Hydrozoa)', *The Biological Bulletin* 190:3 (1996), 302–12, p. 309.
33 Ibid.
34 Ibid., p. 303.
35 Ibid., p. 309.
36 Ibid., p. 302.
37 Ibid., p. 310.
38 Braun, 'Reflections on the Phenomenon of Rejuvenescence in Nature', p. 9.
39 Plato, *Protagoras*, trans. Stanley Lombardo and Karen Bell (Indianapolis: Hackett, 1992), p. 16 (321c).
40 Ibid., p. 17 (322a).
41 Johann Wolfgang von Goethe, *The Metamorphosis of Plants* (Cambridge, MA: MIT Press, 2009), pp. 5–6.
42 Carl Linnaeus, *Linnaeus' Philosophia Botanica*, trans. Stephen Freer (Oxford: Oxford University Press, 2003), pp. 334–5.
43 Caspar Friedrich Wolff, 'De formatione intestinorum praecipue, tum et de amnio spurio aliisque partibus embryonis gallinacei, nondum visis, observationes in ovis incubatis institutae', in *Novi Commentarii Academiae Scientiarum Imperialis Petropolitanae* (Petropoli Typis Academiae Scientiarum, 20 vols, 1747–75), vol. 13, 478–530, p. 410.
44 Ibid., p. 409.
45 Ibid., p. 410.
46 Goethe, *Metamorphosis of Plants*, pp. 99–100.
47 Ibid., p. 100.
48 Nils Ericsson Dahlberg, *Metamorphosis plantarum* (Stockholm: E Typographia Regia, 1755), p. 7.

49 Ibid., p. 10.
50 Swammerdam, *Book of Nature*, p. 9.
51 Ibid.
52 'Outline for a General Introduction to Comparative Anatomy' (1795). [Only an excerpt from Goethe's essay, not including this passage, has been translated into English; it appears in Douglas Miller (ed.), *Goethe: Scientific Studies* (New York: Suhrkamp, 1988), pp. 117–26 – trans.]
53 Ibid.

3 REINCARNATIONS

1 Val Plumwood, *The Eye of the Crocodile* (Canberra: Australian National University, 2012), p. 12.
2 Ibid., p. 13.
3 Ibid., p. 18.
4 Ibid., p. 12.
5 Ibid., p. 16.
6 Ibid., p. 14.
7 Ibid., p. 15.
8 Ibid.
9 Ibid., p. 18.
10 Ibid., pp. 18, 20.
11 Ibid., p. 13.
12 Ibid., p. 80.
13 Ibid.
14 Ovid, *Metamorphoses*, trans. A.D. Melville (Oxford: Oxford World's Classics, 1986), p. 359.
15 Ibid., p. 365.
16 Ibid., p. 357.
17 Aldo Leopold, 'Odyssey', in *A Sand County Almanac and Sketches Here and There* (Oxford: Oxford University Press, 1949), pp. 104–8.
18 Ibid., p. 104.
19 Ibid., p. 107.

20 Ibid.
21 Ibid., p. 108.
22 Ibid., p. 107.
23 Adelbert von Chamisso, *Peter Schlemihl*, trans. Sir John Bowring (London: Robert Hardwicke, 1861), p. 122.
24 Adelbert von Chamisso, *Werke, Zweite Auflage, V Band, Leben und Briefe von Adelbert von Chamisso, hrsg von Julius Eduard Hitzig, Erster Band* (Leipzig: Weidmann'sche Buchhandlung, 1842), p. 271.
25 Adelbert von Chamisso's *Werke, Erster Band, Reise um die Welt, ersther Theil* (Leipzig : Weidmann'sche Buchhandlung 1836), p. 51.
26 Ibid.
27 Adelbert von Chamisso, *De animalibus quibusdam e classe vermium Linnaeana in circumnavigatione Terrae: De Salpa* (Berlin: F. Dümler, 1819), p. 3.
28 M. Sars, 'Über die Entwicklung der *Medusa aurita* (Ohrenqualle) und der *Cyanea capillata*', *Archiv für Naturgeschichte* 7, 1841, ed. von W. F. Erichson, 9–34, p. 29.
29 J.J.S. Steenstrup, *Ueber den Generationswechsel oder die Fortpflanzung und Entwickelung durch abwechselnde Generationen, eine eigenthümliche Form der Brutpflege in den niederen Thierclassen* (Copenhagen, 1842), p. VVI.
30 Ibid., p. VI.
31 Sir Richard Owen, 'On Metamorphosis and Metagenesis', *Notices of the Meetings of the Royal Institution* (7 February 1851), 9–16, p. 11.
32 Steenstrup, *Ueber den Generationswechsel*, p. 118.
33 Ibid.

4 MIGRATIONS

1 Plato, *Timaeus*, trans. Donald J. Zeyl (Indianapolis: Hackett, 2000), p. 29.
2 Ernst Haeckel, *Generelle Morphologie der Organismen: Allgemeine Grundzüge der organischen Formen-Wissenschaft, mechanisch begründet durch die von Charles Darwin reformierte Deszendenz-Theorie* (Berlin: G. Reimer, 1866), vol. 2, pp. 235–6.
3 Ibid., p. 236.
4 Frederic Clements and Victor Shelford, *Bio-Ecology* (New York: Wiley, 1939), p. 3.
5 Haeckel, *Generelle Morphologie der Organismen*, vol. 2, p. 234.
6 Ibid.
7 Ibid., pp. 234–5.
8 Claude Lévi-Strauss, *The Savage Mind* (London: Weidenfeld & Nicolson, 1966), p. 104.
9 Isaak Biberg, *Specimen Academicum de Oeconomia Naturae* (Uppsala, 1749), p. 3.
10 Aristotle, *Oikonomika*, 1343a.
11 Xenophon, *The Economist*, trans. H.G. Dakyns, gutenberg.org, VI.4.
12 Ibid. [translation modified].
13 Christopher Eliasson Gedner, *Quaestio historico naturalis: cui bono?* (Uppsala, 1752), p. 27.
14 Isaak Biberg, *Specimen Academicum de Oeconomia Naturae* (Uppsala, 1749), p. 3.
15 Christoph D. Wilcke, *De Politia Naturae* (Uppsala, 1760), pp. 1–2.
16 Henri Lecoq, *Étude sur la géographie botanique de l'Europe, et, en particulier, sur la végétation du plateau central de la France* (Paris: Baillière et Fils, 8 vols, 1854–58), vol. I, p. xi.
17 Ibid.
18 H.C. Watson, *The New Botanist's Guide to the*

Localities of the Rarer Plants of Britain (London: Longman, 1835), p. 38.

19 H.C. Watson, *Cybele Britannica* (London: Longman, 4 vols, 1847), vol. 1, p. 62.

5 ASSOCIATIONS

1 William Cronon, *Nature's Metropolis: Chicago and the Great West* (New York: W.W. Norton, 1991), p. 19.

2 Paul Shepard, *Thinking Animals: Animals and the Development of Human Intelligence* (Atlanta: University of Georgia Press, 1998).

3 Richard O. Prum, *The Evolution of Beauty: How Darwin's Forgotten Theory of Mate Choice Shapes the Animal World – and Us* (New York: Doubleday, 2017).

4 Lévi-Strauss, *The Savage Mind*, p. 3.

5 Ibid., p. 13.

6 Ibid., p. 3.

7 William Cronon, 'The Trouble with Wilderness; or, Getting Back to the Wrong Nature', in William Cronon (ed.), *Uncommon Ground: Rethinking the Human Place in Nature* (New York: W.W. Norton, 1995), pp. 69–90.

CONCLUSION

1 Eduardo Viveiros de Castro, *Cannibal Metaphysics: For a Post-Structural Anthropology*, trans. Peter Skafish (Minneapolis: Univocal, 2014).